HUMAN BODY II

Britannica Illustrated Science Library

Encyclopædia Britannica, Inc.
Chicago ■ London ■ New Delhi ■ Paris ■ Seoul ■ Sydney ■ Taipei ■ Tokyo

Britannica Illustrated Science Library

Idea and Concept of This Work: Editorial Sol 90

Project Management: Fabián Cassan

Photo Credits: Corbis, ESA, Getty Images, Graphic News, NASA, National Geographic, Science Photo Library

Illustrators: Guido Arroyo, Pablo Aschei, Carlos Francisco Bulzomi, Gustavo J. Caironi, Hernán Cañellas, Leonardo César, José Luis Corsetti, Vanina Farías, Manrique Fernández Buente, Joana Garrido, Celina Hilbert, Inkspot, Jorge Ivanovich, Iván Longuini, Isidro López, Diego Martín, Jorge Martínez, Marco Menco, Marcelo Morán, Ala de Mosca, Diego Mourelos, Laura Mourelos, Pablo Palastro, Eduardo Pérez, Javier Pérez, Ariel Piroyansky, Fernando Ramallo, Ariel Roldán, Marcel Socías, Néstor Taylor, Trebol Animation, Juan Venegas, Constanza Vicco, Coralia Vignau, Gustavo Yamin, 3DN, 3DOM studio

Composition and Pre-press Services: Editorial Sol 90
Translation Services and Index: Publication Services, Inc.

Britannica Illustrated Science Library Staff

Editorial
Michael Levy, *Executive Editor, Core Editorial*
John Rafferty, *Associate Editor, Earth Sciences*
William L. Hosch, *Associate Editor, Mathematics and Computers*
Kara Rogers, *Associate Editor, Life Sciences*
Rob Curley, *Senior Editor, Science and Technology*
David Hayes, *Special Projects Editor*

Art and Composition
Steven N. Kapusta, *Director*
Carol A. Gaines, *Composition Supervisor*
Christine McCabe, *Senior Illustrator*

Media Acquisition
Kathy Nakamura, *Manager*

Copy Department
Sylvia Wallace, *Director*
Julian Ronning, *Supervisor*

Information Management and Retrieval
Sheila Vasich, *Information Architect*

Production Control
Marilyn L. Barton

Manufacturing
Kim Gerber, *Director*

Encyclopædia Britannica, Inc.

Jacob E. Safra, *Chairman of the Board*

Jorge Aguilar-Cauz, *President*

Michael Ross, *Senior Vice President, Corporate Development*

Dale H. Hoiberg, *Senior Vice President and Editor*

Marsha Mackenzie, *Director of Production*

International Standard Book Number (set):
978-1-59339-382-3
International Standard Book Number (volume):
978-1-59339-391-5
Britannica Illustrated Science Library: Human Body II 2008

Printed in China

ENCYCLOPÆDIA
Britannica

www.britannica.com

Human Body II

Contents

The Miracle of Life

This is a moving book. A guide for parents as well as young people, it recounts in detail the almost magical way in which babies evolve from the very moment that fertilization occurs. Thanks to new technological advances, today it is possible to visualize and re-create images of what happens inside a woman's body when a sperm travels through the uterus and the gelatinous membrane that surrounds the egg. Incredible photos show, day by day, how the embryo evolves, when the heart begins to beat, and even when the brain, eyes, legs, arms, mouth, and teeth are formed. This book contains a wealth of information, with photographic details that show you the inside of the body from a totally new viewpoint.

The book is divided into five chapters. The first two are dedicated to the formation and development of the baby, and the rest deal with everything that happens to the body when it gets sick—from how the HIV/AIDS virus affects us to what happens when arteries become blocked because of fat deposits. The information, reviewed by professionals and accompanied by incredible illustrations, will captivate you from the first page. The last chapter is devoted to tracing the landscape of future medicine. The surprising advances in molecular biology and genetics allow us to have new therapeutic and diagnostic tools that make it possible to think that, in the future, humans will live eternally. The themes covered and shown here have a scientific basis. We tell you, for example, which mechanisms regulate the operation of the genes and how these mechanisms can correct certain errors in the DNA—the starting point for many illnesses of genetic origin, including many forms of cancer. In a not too distant future, nanomachines (many times smaller than a cell) could be guided inside the body to eliminate obstructions in blood vessels or to kill cancer cells. With particles the size of amino acids, sick cells could be eliminated without damaging the healthy ones. Like guided missiles, the molecules would go directly to the damaged cells. This type of therapy has already been demonstrated in mice and rats, and, although the tests are still in development, it is expected that within the next few years this type of revolutionary treatment, which combines genetics with pharmacology, could be applied. Currently there are patients on whom certain drugs have toxic effects or do not have the desired effect; in the future, drugs could be made according to the genetic makeup of each patient.

Another aspect to highlight in the use of new technologies is related to health informatics, or medical informatics, in which all kinds of patient information is managed. Such a system already allows all hospitals in some cities, such as Vienna, Austria, to communicate digitally. That way a doctor can quickly access the medical record of the person through a remote communication network such as the Internet. It is not strange to imagine that in coming years everyone will carry their medical records on a keychain that, when connected to a computer, would provide all their medical information. There is real evidence that in the next decades the way that medicine will treat diseases requiring the replacement of organs or tissues will also change. The tissue created in the laboratory will be genetically identical to the patient's, so there will be no rejection. Once this is achieved, transplants and artificial organ implants will be a thing of the past. Today in the cases of heart failure, when the treatments do not work, a transplant is sought. In a few more years, this will be unnecessary. Ventricular assistance devices, combined with stem-cell implants, will be used to allow regeneration of the damaged muscle.

In addition, the health of many people will be determined during fetal development. As a result of the advances in prenatal diagnostic methods, the possibility has appeared in recent years of carrying out surgical procedures to correct certain congenital problems inside the womb. It is not difficult to foresee the development of medical units in which the fetus is a patient. Even though many of these advances are still in the research stage, it is not unrealistic to believe that they will end up being useful. Several decades ago, nobody would have thought about replacing sick organs with healthy ones or the possibility of choosing a baby's sex. So why not fantasize about virtual medicine that is safer, simpler, and more effective or even about the possibility of living forever? ●

From Zygote to Embryo

From conception until the third month of pregnancy, what takes place inside the mother's belly? Day by day, during the phases of mitosis, what happens at this embryonic stage, the most critical one during pregnancy? What changes does the embryo go through? Here we present incredible images that show the embryo from its formation to the moment it

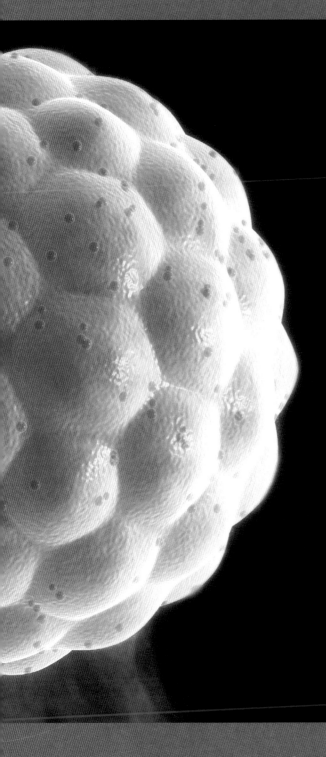

implants itself in the endometrium and measures about 0.2 inch (5 mm). At what time do the heartbeats begin and the eyes, mouth, and legs begin to form? Also, what is the role of the placenta, the organ that gives the unborn baby the different nutrients and oxygen it needs to continue developing? Turn the page. ●

The Origin of Sex and Life

The origin of human reproduction is sexual. Men and women can have sex any time during the year, unlike most other species, which have their specific times of heat. The ability to have sex begins at puberty, the age when the sexual organs develop. Women are fertile from their first menstrual period until menopause at around age 45. Although their sexual activity continues after this age, they no longer produce eggs, the female sexual gametes capable of being fertilized by sperm. ●

The Male Sexual Apparatus

The testicles, or male sexual glands, lie below the pelvis within a structure called the scrotum. It is there that sperm—the mobile sex cells—are produced. During sexual intercourse, these cells, if they reach the female vaginal canal, head toward the egg so that one of them may fertilize it. The ductus deferens is the path through which the sperm travels to be joined by materials from the seminal vesicles and the prostate. This combination makes up the semen, which, in the moments of maximum sexual excitation, will move to the urethra to exit the man's body through the penis.

Gametes and Hormones

Testicles and ovaries are glands that produce the sex cells, or gametes—sperm and eggs, respectively. Gametes are haploid cells. In other words, they possess half the chromosomes of any other human tissue cell, which contains a total of 46. Upon uniting at conception, each gamete contributes half of the genetic load of the new embryo. The sex glands also produce hormones that determine secondary characteristics and, in women, ovulation.

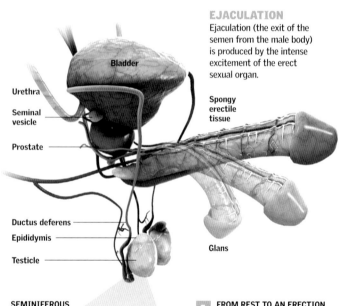

EJACULATION
Ejaculation (the exit of the semen from the male body) is produced by the intense excitement of the erect sexual organ.

Bladder

Urethra

Seminal vesicle

Prostate

Ductus deferens

Epididymis

Testicle

Spongy erectile tissue

Glans

FALLOPIAN TUBE
A tube 4 to 5 inches (10-12 cm) in length and about 0.1 inch (3 mm) in diameter, with internal cilia that propel the egg toward the uterus.

FIMBRIAE
form a tunnel through which the mature egg is introduced into the fallopian tubes.

28
DAYS A TYPICAL MENSTRUAL CYCLE LASTS

OVARY
contains many follicles with immature eggs and releases hormones responsible for the menstrual cycle and female sexual activity.

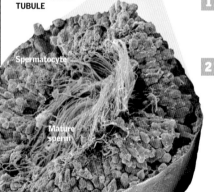

SEMINIFEROUS TUBULE

Spermatocyte

Mature sperm

Spermatid

1 FROM REST TO AN ERECTION
A physical or mental stimulus causes the cavernous bodies to fill with blood and the penis to swell.

2 EJACULATION
If the penis continues being stimulated, the seminal vesicle contracts and expels the semen.

SPERM PRODUCTION
Sperm originates inside the 10,000 seminiferous tubules at a rate of 120 million a day and are stored in the epididymis. This process requires a temperature of 93° F (34° C), which the testicles achieve by being outside the abdomen.

FRONT VIEW

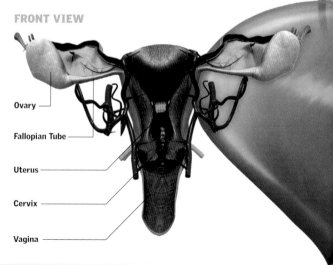

Ovary

Fallopian Tube

Uterus

Cervix

Vagina

The Menstrual Cycle

The uterus is prepared for the implantation of the fertilized egg. For this, the woman's hormones have stimulated the uterus to thicken its internal wall (endometrium). If no egg is implanted, the thickened wall breaks down and the waste material is disposed of outside the body, together with the unfertilized egg. This process is synchronized with ovulation and is repeated regularly throughout the woman's fertile life, from puberty until menopause.

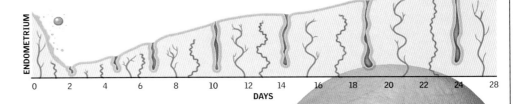

Menstruation
The female body disposes of the dead cells from the endometrium.

Thickening
The blood vessels of the uterus lengthen, and the wall grows.

Maximum hormone levels
Estrogen, luteinizing hormone (LH), and follicle-stimulating hormone (FSH)

Ovulation
occurs around the 14th day after menstruation.

Increase in progesterone
The hormone that prepares the endometrium for implantation

Arrival of the egg
If it is fertilized, it becomes implanted; if not, menstruation occurs.

ENDOMETRIUM

0 2 4 6 8 10 12 14 16 18 20 22 24 28

DAYS

The Sexual Organs of the Woman

With the exception of the vulva, which is external, the female sexual apparatus (which allows a woman to have an active sexual life, become pregnant, and give birth) lies completely inside the abdominal cavity, where it is supported and protected by the pelvis. Its basic shape is that of a cavity formed by the vagina and the uterus. The ovaries produce the eggs, or sex cells, and hormones. Periodically a mature egg leaves the ovary and installs itself in the uterus (ovulation). There, if it has not been fertilized in the fallopian tube, the body will expel it naturally together with the residues of the endometrium (menstruation).

OVULATION CYCLE
Inside the ovary there are thousands of immature eggs, each one wrapped in a follicle, or sac. In each cycle, a mature egg is sent to the uterus.

UTERUS
A pear-shaped cavity with thick, muscular walls. Its internal wall is the endometrium.

BLADDER

VAGINA
Cavity that is anatomically prepared to receive the penis during sexual intercourse

1 The egg begins to grow in a follicle, stimulated by FSH.

2 Protection
The follicular cells form an envelope around the egg.

3 Maturing of the egg
The egg bulges from the ovarian walls, and hormonal secretions increase.

4 Maximum size
The follicle has formed a fluid-filled cavity.

5 Ovulation
Halfway through the cycle, the follicle bursts and releases a mature egg.

6 Formation of the corpus luteum
The ruptured follicle closes and releases progesterone.

7 Degeneration of the corpus luteum
occurs only if the egg has not been fertilized.

Fertilization of the Egg

ertilization is the starting point for the development of pregnancy. After intercourse, two sex cells, or gametes, fuse together, giving rise to an ovum, or zygote, where the chromosomes of the two gametes are united. In humans, these sex cells are the sperm and the egg. For conception of a new life, a sperm must fertilize the egg in a tough competition with hundreds of millions of other sperm.

The Journey of a Sperm

After ejaculation, millions of sperm begin their journey through the genital tract. Only 200 will reach the egg. The trip toward the fallopian tubes takes anywhere from 15 minutes to several hours. To reach them, sperm use their tails, and they are helped by contractions in the walls of the vagina and the uterus. Inside the egg, the sperm loses its tail and midsection, which dissolve. The head, which contains the genetic material, moves toward the plasma membrane of the egg. The march toward fertilization is underway.

ZONA PELLUCIDA
Thick, translucent layer outside the cell membrane. It is penetrated by the sperm.

CELL MEMBRANE
protects the egg. The sperm goes through it after passing through the zona pellucida.

FROM PENETRATION TO FERTILIZATION

ENLARGED AREA

Fallopian Tube

Uterus

Ovary

3 Fertilization
In the fallopian tubes, a sperm fertilizes the egg.

Cervix

2 Ejaculation
250 million sperm are released into the vagina.

Vagina

250

MILLION SPERM
begin their journey through the genital tract after ejaculation. Only one will fertilize the egg.

1 Penetration
The erect penis enters the widened and moistened vagina.

Penis

2 Only One Winner

The sperm that will finally fertilize the egg will release enzymes that allow it to cros through the external membranes of the egg. Wher it enters, it loses its tail and midsection. What remains in the egg is the head with the genetic material.

The Sperm

The male sex cell. With a tail, a head, and a midsection, millions of sperm fight to fertilize the egg, a mission that only one of them will accomplish. It measures 0.002 inch (0.05 mm) in length.

MIDSECTION
contains mitochondria that release energy to move the tail.

HEAD
contains the genetic information (DNA).

TAIL
helps the sperm move through the external membranes of the egg.

1 In the Race

Hundreds of millions of sperm go in search of the egg immediately after ejaculation during reproduction.

Day 1

4 Mitosis

The process of generating new cells. Cell division begins with the replication of the DNA. In this way, a "mother" cell generates two identical "daughter" cells that contain the same genetic information as the mother cell. The process of replication for cell division occurs for each of the 46 chromosomes in each cell. The cells of the embryo divide through mitosis, just like most adult tissue cells.

PHASES OF MITOSIS

1 Prophase
The DNA of the chromosomes has already been copied. Two identical strands are formed, joined at the center by a structure called a centromere.

Nucleus
Cytoplasm
Centromere
Chromatin
Sister Chromatids

Filament   **Centriole**

2 Metaphase
The membrane that covers the cell nucleus disappears, and filaments form in the cell. The chromosomes align themselves along these filaments across the middle of the cell.

Daughter chromosomes

3 Fertilization

A zygote, or ovum, is produced from the union of the egg and the sperm. The cell will begin its cell division through mitosis.

3 Anaphase
The filaments "tug" the duplicated chromosomes. The duplicated individual chromosomes move toward the two ends of the cell.

NUCLEUS OF THE EGG contains the genetic material made up of DNA.

4 Telophase
The filaments disappear, and a new nuclear envelope forms around each group of 46 chromosomes. The nucleus has divided in two.

The Egg

When the egg is fertilized by a sperm, pregnancy starts. Fertilization occurs in the exterior portion of the fallopian tube where the sperm meets and joins with the egg. Two days after fertilization, the egg travels toward the uterus, pushed along by the muscular action of the fallopian tube. The egg, once fertilized, thickens its outer surface to prevent the entrance of any new sperm. After fertilization, the zygote begins to divide through mitosis.

5 Late telophase
The new cells have been formed. The daughter cells contain the same genetic material as the original cell.

0.1 inch (3 mm)
DISTANCE SPERM TRAVELS IN A MINUTE

Zona pellucida

A membrane of glycoproteins that surrounds the plasma membrane of an oocyte, a female sex cell. This structure attracts the sperm and is vital for the release of the sperm head. In humans, the membrane degenerates and breaks down five days after fertilization.

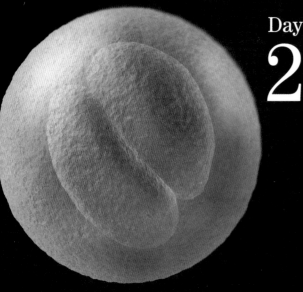

Day 2

Formation of the Morula

The zygote goes through three stages of cell division. While it travels through the fallopian tube, it divides first into two and then into four identical cells. After 72 hours, it will have reached the stage of 16 cells, at which point a mulberry-shaped cell agglomerate called the morula is formed (the name comes from the Latin word morum, meaning "mulberry"). The morula continues its journey through the fallopian tube until it reaches the uterus. Cell division continues until a more solid ball with 64 cells, the blastocyst, is formed. Once the blastocyst attaches itself to the interior of the uterus, the formation of the embryo begins.

X-ray of the morula

The morula is made up of 16 cells in its initial state. As it divides, it will reach 64 cells, at which time it becomes a blastocyst.

BLASTOMERES
Small cells that make up the body of the morula

MEMBRANE
covers the cellular mass; made up of proteins.

LIQUID
Fluid develops within the intercellular spaces.

Zygote

The resultant cell from the union of the male gamete (sperm) with the female gamete (egg) in sexual reproduction is called the zygote. Its cytoplasm and organelles are from the maternal egg. It contains all the necessary genetic material for fetal development.

0.004 inch (0.1 mm)

DIAMETER OF THE ZYGOTE

Morula

The second important stage of development prior to the formation of the blastocyst. It forms from the repeated mitosis of the zygote. Initially its interior contains 16 blastomeres, which are the first cells that develop from the zygote. Inside the morula, these cells are uniform in shape, size, and physiological potential.

Fertilization

Fertilization occurs in the upper part of the fallopian tube. When the head of the sperm penetrates a mature egg, the nuclei of both sex cells, each one with 23 chromosomes, fuse to form the zygote, or ovum. With 46 chromosomes, the zygote will begin the process of successive cell divisions through mitosis. It will begin the journey from the fallopian tubes toward the endometrium, where it will implant itself.

12 hours

How long it takes the zygote, or ovum, to divide through mitosis. Compact masses are successively formed in these cellular multiplications.

The Zygote's Journey

Once the sex cells have formed the zygote, it begins the journey toward the uterus through the fallopian tube. During this journey, several cellular divisions will take place. Before entering the uterine cavity, a mulberry-shaped compact cellular mass is formed (the morula). Within the uterus, cellular divisions take place every 12 hours until the blastocyst stage (about 64 cells) has been reached. Once on the uterine lining, the blastocyst adheres to it, and shortly thereafter implantation takes place. From that moment, embryonic growth begins.

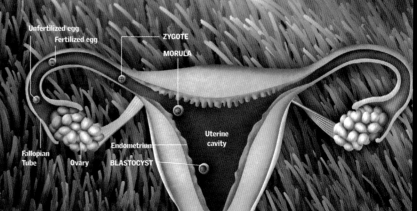

Unfertilized egg
Fertilized egg
ZYGOTE
MORULA
Uterine cavity
Fallopian Tube
Ovary
Endometrium
BLASTOCYST

9 days

AFTER FERTILIZATION

The blastocyst, the stage prior to the embryonic stage, implants itself in the uterine wall.

Implantation

After cellular division to 64 cells, the morula becomes a blastocyst, a more compact and solid mass. Once formed, the blastocyst moves freely in the uterine cavity for 48 hours before finding a place to implant itself in the endometrium. The endometrium relaxes to ease implantation of the blastocyst. Nine days after fertilization, the embryo will already be in the uterine wall. After implantation, the embryo begins to grow. If the woman has very low levels of estrogen and progesterone, the endometrium can rupture and cause implantation to occur in the wrong place.

Day 4

Blastocyst

The last step before growth of the embryo. The cellular mass is covered with an external layer called the trophoblast. The trophoblast releases enzymes that help the blastocyst adhere to the endometrium.

TROPHOBLAST
forms the embryonic part of the placenta.

CAVITY, OR BLASTOCOEL
contains liquid that passes through the zona pellucida from the uterine cavity.

They make up the embryo, or embryoblast.

IT IMPLANTS NINE DAYS AFTER FERTILIZATION.

Day 9

Trilaminar disk

begins to form from the embryonic bilaminar disk and is complete by day 15. From the trilaminar disk, three germinative layers will develop; they will give rise to the distinct parts of the body: mesoderm, endoderm, and ectoderm.

AMNIOTIC CAVITY

PRIMITIVE GROOVE

ECTODERM
is the outermost layer. It develops into skin, hair, fingernails, the central nervous system, parts of the eye, the nasal cavity, and tooth enamel.

MESODERM
forms the bones, muscles, cartilage, connective tissue, heart, blood, blood vessels, lymphatic cells, lymphatic vessels, and various glands.

YOLK SAC

ENDODERM
is the innermost layer. It forms the lining of the digestive and respiratory tracts, liver ducts, pancreatic ducts, and glands such as the thyroid gland and the salivary gland.

The Endometrium

The inner layer of the uterine wall, it is made up of the myometrium—the external musculature—and the endometrium—the internal mucosa. Its function is to receive the ovum for implantation. When there is no pregnancy, the endometrium is the bloody tissue lost during menstruation.

First Human Forms

Nine days after fertilization, the blastocyst has installed itself in the wall of the uterine endometrium, where it will spend the rest of the nine months of gestation before being born. The blastocyst measures slightly more than 0.004 inch (0.1 mm), and the uterine wall increases in size and attains a spongy consistency, the product of an intense supply of hormones by the ovaries. The uterine wall is where the stages of embryonic development will continue. The formation of the various kinds of tissues begins, and in the third week, the heartbeat starts. ●

Protective Membrane

The rubbing of the blastocyst against the zona pellucida of the endometrium (normally in the back of the uterus, the part closest to the spine) leads to the release of enzymes that interact with the embryo. The blastocyst has little trouble penetrating the porous wall. At the same time, a new membrane forms: the chorion, which will protect the embryo.

Cellular Differentiation

Inside the embryo are cells that will form the skeleton as well as cells that will make up the viscera. Originally undifferentiated, they begin to move, seeking their place. Some cells will move outward (those that will form the skeleton) and others inward (those that will make up the viscera). The latest research has shown that some cells release certain chemicals that provoke other cells to do certain tasks. These substances are called morphogens.

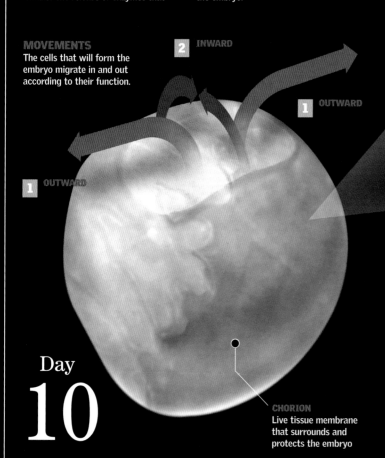

MOVEMENTS
The cells that will form the embryo migrate in and out according to their function.

2 INWARD

1 OUTWARD

1 OUTWARD

Day
10

CHORION
Live tissue membrane that surrounds and protects the embryo

1 First, the cells related to skeleton formation migrate toward the outside. They place themselves on the wall of the embryo.

2 Soon after, the cells related to visceral growth begin to migrate toward the inside. The embryonic disk undergoes a transformation.

Morphogenesis

includes the formation of the tissues and organs of the embryo. In this process, the cells are distributed along specific sites according to the tissues or organs they will form.

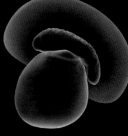

Day
13

CHANGES IN SHAPE
When the cells that will form the viscera find their place, the embryo undergoes a transformation within a few hours. From the disklike appearance of day 13, a tube forms from filaments that are generated by these cells.

The Placenta Forms

From the implanted blastocyst, new cellular formations begin to branch out over the chorion. These branches (called trophoblasts) are the source of the placenta, a disk-shaped interchange organ that grows between the chorion and the tissues of the endometrium. In the placenta, the blood vessels of the mother intertwine with those of the embryo without joining. The embryoblast, which contains the source of primitive blood for the development of the liver and the marrow, grows under this disk, which serves as a protective and immunological barrier.

1,000 cells

MAKE UP THE HUMAN EMBRYO BY THE TIME THE PLACENTA IS FORMED (DAY 13) AND GASTRULATION BEGINS.

Day 19

8 inches (20 cm)

is the average diameter of the placenta responsible for blood circulation between the mother and the fetus at the time of birth.

87 gallons (330 L) A DAY

The amount of blood that must circulate through the umbilical cord to sustain embryonic growth.

Organic Foundation

After different cell migrations and their installation in specific places, the foundation is laid for the integral construction of a new being. The neural tube has acquired its shape and will be key in the formation of the nervous system. The heart is in its place and in a few days will begin to beat.

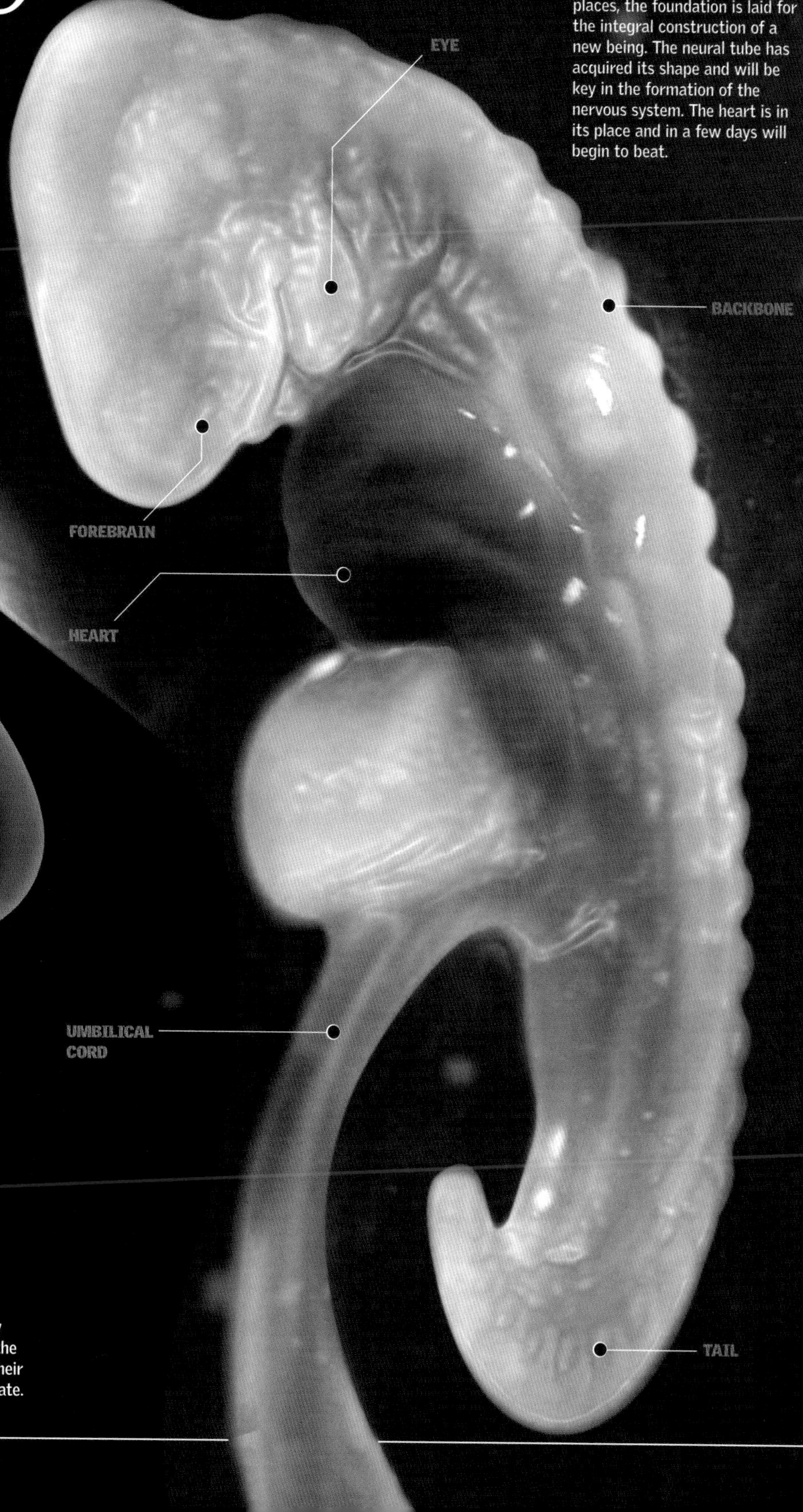

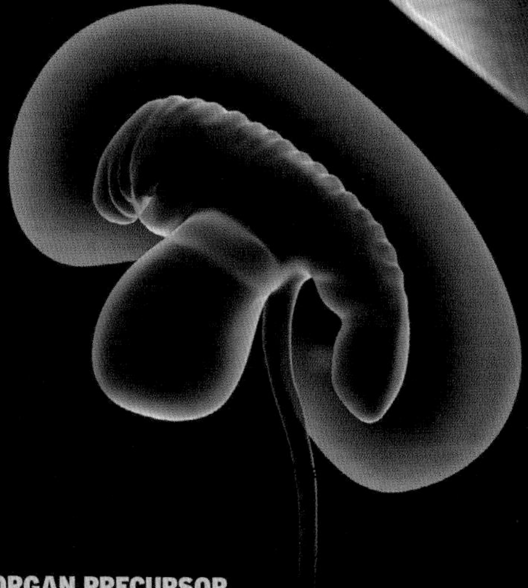

EYE

BACKBONE

FOREBRAIN

HEART

ORGAN PRECURSOR

Between days 16 and 19, the neuroblasts appear and the neural tube forms. These cells possess information to generate the brain and the rest of the nervous system. The three folds that arise during neural tube development later possess sensory and motor function. At the time of neural tube development, blood vessels appear.

UMBILICAL CORD

Stem Cells

The cells that make up the blastocysts are not differentiated, and they contain all the information necessary to generate from themselves every tissue that will make up the human body. It is this capacity that distinguishes these cells as stem cells. To form the various tissues, these cells lose or suppress part of their genetic information as they reproduce and differentiate.

TAIL

Embryonic Stage

It is still impossible to see a human shape at this moment of intrauterine development. The embryo is smaller than a grain of rice and has at one end a type of curved tail that will disappear as development progresses. In the interior and in the folds of the embryo there are groups of various cells, each one with different instructions according to the organs they must form. In this period, the cells of the cardiovascular system initiate the beating of the heart.

Day
22

LENGTH: 0.2 inch (4 mm)
WEIGHT: 0.001 ounce (0.03 g)

ESOPHAGUS
separates from the breathing tube to allow the appropriate development of the digestive system.

LUNGS
begin to develop. They are the last organs to acquire their shape and be completely functional.

SPINE
has 40 pairs of muscles and 33 pairs of vertebrae. It is the hardest part of the embryo.

Liver and Kidneys

During the embryonic period, the first two months of gestation, the liver is the central organ for blood production. It is in charge of producing blood cells because the bone marrow, the substance that will have this function with the beginning of the fetal period, is not yet complete. In addition, the primitive kidneys begin to appear in the embryo from a protuberance called the mesonephric ridge. The kidneys filter the metabolic waste from the blood so that the embryo receives only the nutrients.

C-shaped

In most vertebrates, the curved C-shape will disappear as the body slowly grows.

1 FOLD
The embryonic tail acquires a curved shaped before its disappearance.

2 ABSORPTION
The tail is absorbed when the embryo begins the road to fetal development.

127 million

The average number of cells in the eye when it acquires its definitive shape.

Formation of the Eye

All vertebrates' eyes develop according to the same process. From certain changes in the ectodermal layer and invagination patterns on the surface of the embryo, the eye develops an "inverted" retina, in which the initial detection of light rays occurs in the outermost portion. In this way, the light-sensitive elements are situated on the outer regions, and the neural connection with the brain is in the inner region. The retina houses in its interior light-sensitive cells that have the function of receiving light and transmitting the correct information to the brain. The final development in the eye's functionality will occur at approximately the seventh month, when the baby will open its eyes for the first time and will react to changes of shade between light and dark.

DEVELOPMENT OF THE EYE

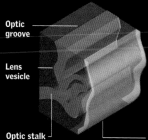

Optic groove
Lens vesicle
Optic stalk
Lens placode

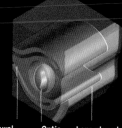

Neural retina
Optic cup
Lens placode

CROSS SECTION

THE EYE WILL BE ABLE TO DISTINGUISH BETWEEN

10 million

COLORS AND SHADES OF LIGHT AND DARK WHEN IT REACHES MAXIMUM DEVELOPMENT.

 DEVELOPMENT OF THE PLACODE
By day 30, the lens placode, a region on the embryonic surface, comes in contact with the optic stalk.

2 FORMATION OF THE VESICLE
A day later, invagination of the lens placode takes place, and the lens vesicle forms.

3 DEVELOPMENT OF THE RETINA
On day 32, the neural retina and the pigment epithelium are formed. The lens vesicle detaches from the placode.

The Heart Begins to Beat

By day 22, the heart is already active, just like the brain. Its division into subregions has begun, and it now makes up, together with the brain, half the size of the fetus. Initially the heart is simply a pump that maintains the flow of blood in the body and toward the placenta. When the four chambers are developed, the heart acquires the ability to gather the blood from the lungs and distribute it toward the organs throughout the body.

3 BULBUS CORDIS
Composed of three parts: the arterial trunk, the arterial cone, and the primitive right ventricle

Development of the Heart

After the differentiation of the cells that form the blood vessels, the cardiac muscle appears and begins to pump with the beating of its cells.

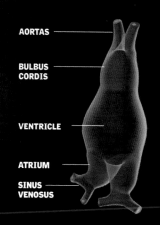

AORTAS
BULBUS CORDIS
VENTRICLE
ATRIUM
SINUS VENOSUS

Upward motion

AORTA
BULBUS CORDIS
ATRIUM
PRIMITIVE LEFT VENTRICLE
SINUS VENOSUS

AMNIOTIC SAC
contains the liquid in which the fetus floats and is made up of two membranes that protect the embryo.

1 GROWTH
The cardiac tube grows and appears divided into different regions separated externally by grooves.

2 FOLDING
Because it is bigger than the cavity that contains it, the primitive structure folds into an S shape.

ENLARGED AREA

50%

of the embryo is composed of just two organs: the heart and the brain.

HEART SURFACE

4 THE CELLS BEAT
The heart cells begin to beat. They all pump blood in unison. The heart has begun to function.

Changes in the Head

The brain, the organ of the central nervous system that coordinates all muscle movement, begins to develop. Inside it, the pituitary gland (hypophysis) begins to form. It will produce growth hormone and other hormones. The jaw and the facial muscles also begin to develop.

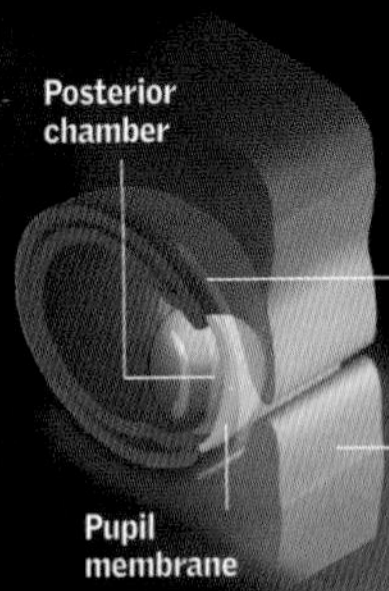

Posterior chamber

Conjunctive sac

EXTERIOR

Eyelid

Pupil membrane

4 EYE
The eyelid forms. A membrane prepares the final shape of the pupil.

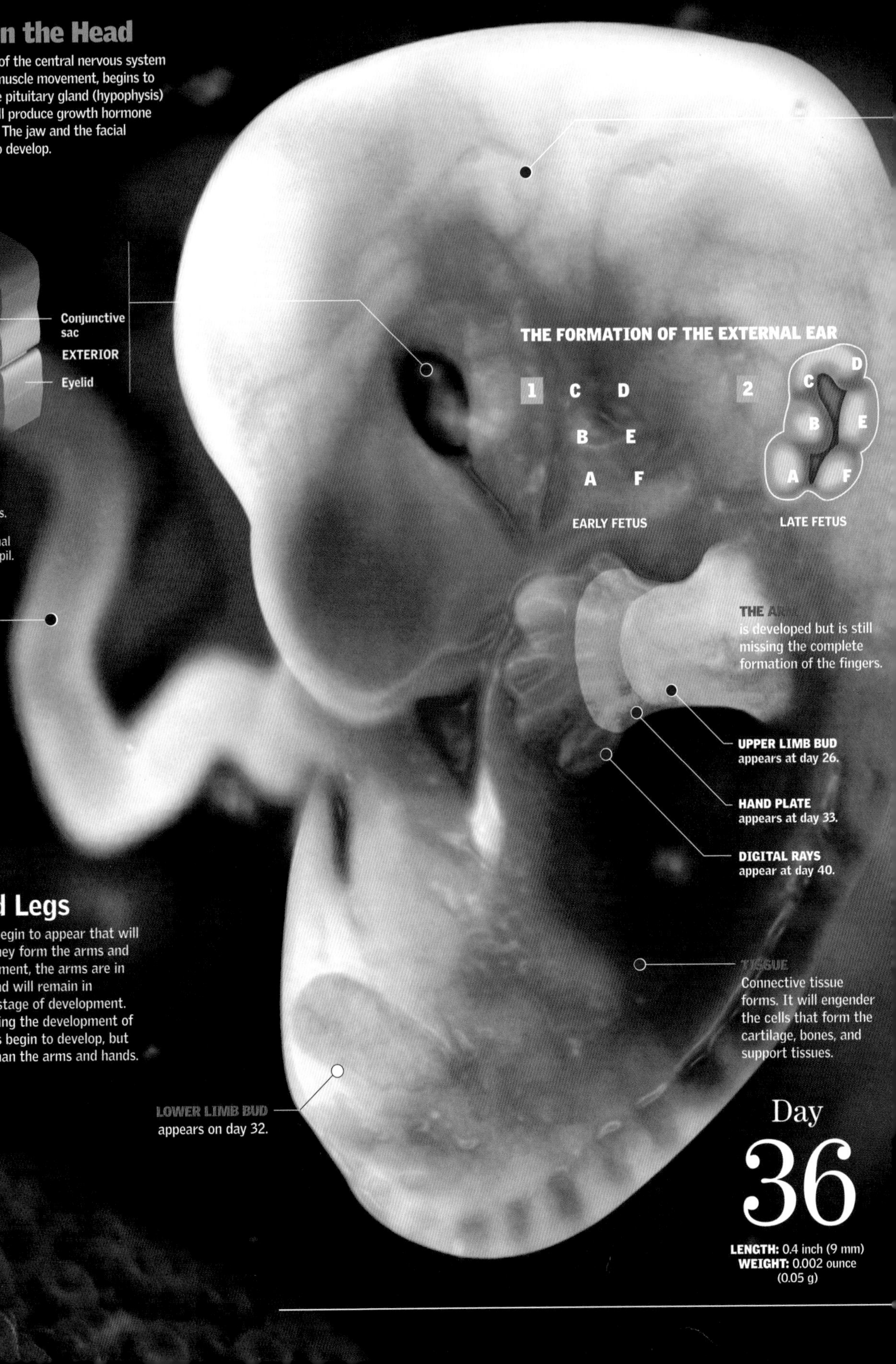

CORD
The umbilical cord begins to develop and, by the time of birth, can measure up to two feet (60 cm) in length.

THE FORMATION OF THE EXTERNAL EAR

1 C D

B E

A F

EARLY FETUS

2 C D

B E

A F

LATE FETUS

THE AR...
is developed but is still missing the complete formation of the fingers.

UPPER LIMB BUD
appears at day 26.

HAND PLATE
appears at day 33.

DIGITAL RAYS
appear at day 40.

Arms and Legs

Small buds begin to appear that will grow until they form the arms and legs. Up to this moment, the arms are in their right place and will remain in proportion to this stage of development. They are only missing the development of the hands. The legs begin to develop, but they take longer than the arms and hands.

TISSUE
Connective tissue forms. It will engender the cells that form the cartilage, bones, and support tissues.

LOWER LIMB BUD
appears on day 32.

Day
36

LENGTH: 0.4 inch (9 mm)
WEIGHT: 0.002 ounce (0.05 g)

THE FOLDS OF THE BRAIN develop as the months of intrauterine life go by.

1 SMOOTH BRAIN
Initially the embryonic brain has a smooth surface.

2 A FEW FOLDS
By six months, some basic folds can be seen.

3 ADULT
The complete folds allow optimal functioning.

Day
40

LENGTH: 0.4 inch (10 mm)
WEIGHT: 0.004 ounce (0.1 g)

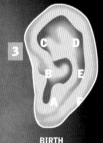

3

BIRTH

The External Ear

▶ Three auricular hillocks can be found in the first arch and three more in the second. As the jaw and teeth develop, the ears move up from the neck toward the sides of the head. Two ectodermic derivations appear in the cephalic region of the embryo: the otic placode and the lens placode. At birth, the external ear exhibits its typical shape.

Eyes

The optical vesicles develop on both sides of the head, move toward the center, and form the eyes, as will the ducts that will make up the inner ear.

GROWTH OF THE FETUS

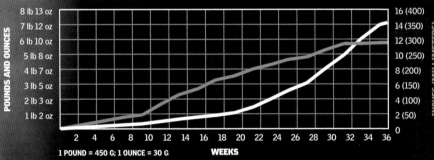

POUNDS AND OUNCES: 8 lb 13 oz, 7 lb 12 oz, 6 lb 10 oz, 5 lb 8 oz, 4 lb 7 oz, 3 lb 5 oz, 2 lb 3 oz, 1 lb 2 oz

INCHES (MILLIMETERS): 16 (400), 14 (350), 12 (300), 10 (250), 8 (200), 6 (150), 4 (100), 2 (50), 0

WEEKS: 2 4 6 8 10 12 14 16 18 20 22 24 26 28 30 32 34 36

1 POUND = 450 G; 1 OUNCE = 30 G

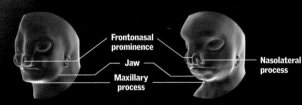

Frontonasal prominence
Jaw
Maxillary process
Nasolateral process

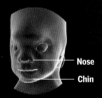

Nose
Chin

FEATURES BECOME DISTINCT

1 Lower jaw
begins to develop by day 37, together with the lips.

2 Nose
is roughed out by the invagination of the frontonasal prominence on day 39.

3 Chin
is already proportional by day 40. The nose has acquired its definitive shape.

Formation of the Face

▶ The facial characteristics are quickly delineated. The pharyngeal arches that surround the stomodeum in the center of the face are configured. The mandibular processes and the frontonasal prominence can already be identified. From the pharyngeal arch, the maxillary process will also develop, which will give rise to the premaxillary, the maxillary, the zygomatic bone, and part of the temporal bone. At the roof of the embryo's mouth, the primitive palate is constructed. Through an invagination in the frontonasal prominence, the nose is shaped. The same thing happens with the chin, which acquires normal proportions by day 40 of intrauterine life.

4 The shape of the face has begun to develop and will continue to do so until the third month.

Day
44

LENGTH: 0.6 inch (16 mm)
WEIGHT: 0.02 ounce (0.5 g)

Changes in the Brain

At this stage, the brain connects with the nervous system. The gland responsible for the production of the hormones begins to develop in it.

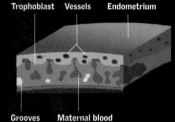

1 FORMATION OF THE PLACENTA
The cells of the trophoblast extend inside the blood vessels of the uterus. The blood from the mother flows from these vessels toward empty spaces inside the trophoblast.

Trophoblast   Vessels   Endometrium

Grooves   Maternal blood

2 THE PLACENTA AS FILTER
The mother's blood and that of the fetus do not have direct contact inside the placenta. They are separated by a barrier of cells. Oxygen, nutrients, and antibodies travel through the barrier and reach the fetus. The waste is returned to the placenta.

Maternal blood   Endometrium

Development of the Placenta

The placenta is a special organ that provides the fetus with different nutrients and oxygen. It also absorbs the waste that the fetus produces and acts as a protective barrier against any harmful substances. The placenta forms from the trophoblast, the external layer of the blastocyst (mass of cells implanted in the uterus after fertilization). It begins to develop after implantation, and by the tent day, it is complete. The placental hormones help preserve the endometrium.

INTERNAL EAR AND MIDDLE EAR

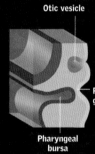

Otic vesicle

Pharyngeal groove

Pharyngeal bursa

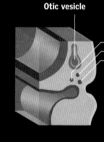

Otic vesicle

Stapes
Anvil
Hammer

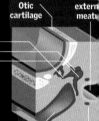

Otic cartilage

Audito extern meat

Tubotympanic recess

Tympan ring

1 22 DAYS
A visible groove appears in the place where the ear will be.

2 28 DAYS
The structures that will give rise to the bones of the middle ear appear.

3 32 DAYS
The middle ear is formed (stapes, anv and hammer).

The Pregnancy Test

A short time after fertilization, the placenta releases a hormone called human chorionic gonadotropin (HCG). The appearance and rapid increase in the concentration of this hormone in the urine are indicators of the existence of a pregnancy. A common pregnancy test contains antibodies that react to the presence of HCG. The user places the tip of the testing device in contact with her urine and waits an indicated amount of time. The presence of two lines in the display will indicate the existence of a pregnancy, while a single line will indicate the opposite. If the test is negative, repeating the test is recommended.

HOW IT WORKS

ABSORPTION OF URINE
An absorbent tip is placed under the urine stream for si seconds, until it is moist.

RESULT
Two lines indicate the presen of pregnancy. If there is only one, it is recommended the test be repeated within 48 to 72 hours.

99%
EFFECTIVE IN DETECTIN
PREGNANCY

3 **END OF THE PLACENTA**
The placenta continues its development as the fetus grows, such that, by the end of the pregnancy, it measures about eight inches (20 cm). It is connected to the baby by the umbilical cord.

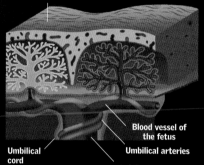

Endometrium

Blood vessel of the fetus

Umbilical cord

Umbilical arteries

Umbilical vein

6 weeks

THE FINGERS APPEAR Although the hand has a shape resembling a small paddle, the digits are becoming distinct.

Membranous labyrinth

Temporal bone

Auditory external meatus

Tympanic membrane

Tympanic cavity

4 **60 DAYS**
The auditory external meatus develops from the pharyngeal groove.

Everything in Place and Working

During this period, the brain and the nervous system develop rapidly. On both sides of the head, the optic vesicles that will make up the eyes have formed, as have the ducts that will make up the inner ear. The heart already beats strongly, and the digestive and respiratory apparatus have begun to take shape. Small buds that will grow to form the arms and legs appear. The fetus, measured from the top of the head to the coccyx, by the sixth week will have reached 0.6 inch (16 mm).

BRAIN
After 51 days, the fourth ventricle of the brain controls the flow of blood, and the circulatory system begins to develop.

THE THALAMUS
The skull begins to form. On day 52, the thalamus develops and can be distinguished. The eyes move toward the front.

THE EAR
begins its development in the fourth week but will not be complete until the sixth month, when it carries out the function of bodily equilibrium.

INTERNAL ORGANS
At this stage, all the essential organs begin to develop in the gastrointestinal, respiratory, and reproductive systems.

Day

60

LENGTH: 1.2 inches (3 cm)
WEIGHT: 0.1 ounce (3 g)

Fetal Development and Childbirth

The fetus's growth continues progressing day by day, and this chapter illustrates the most notable changes that can be seen. By now, it is possible to distinguish ovaries from testicles, to observe the external parts of the ear, and to see the limbs flex. We will also use pictures to tell you about DNA, the key substance of the body that enables

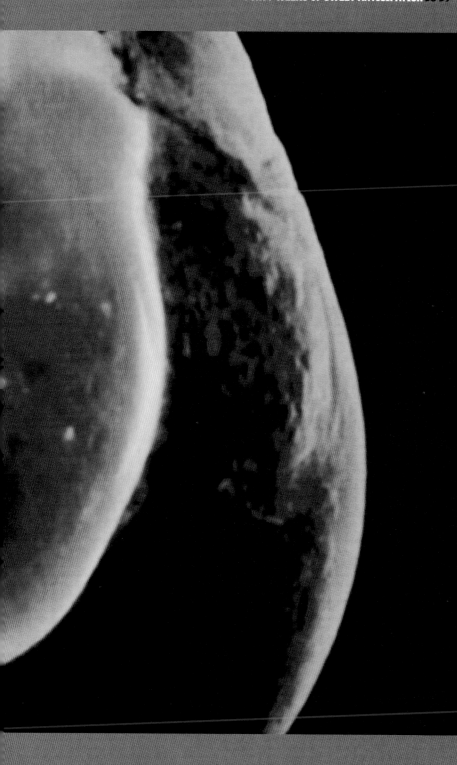

hereditary characteristics to be passed from one generation to the next. Which tests must pregnant women take to find out if fetal development is normal? What are the most notable changes that the woman's body goes through, and what happens once the baby begins to breathe and live outside the womb? ●

Neuron Development

The third month of fetal development brings distinct changes compared with previous stages. What was once called the embryo is now a fetus. The number of neurons in the brain increases rapidly, and toward the end of the month the fetus has the same number of nerve cells as an adult. However, the interneuron connections have not been established. During this month, through nerve impulses, the network will take shape, which in later months will allow voluntary movements of the joints. •

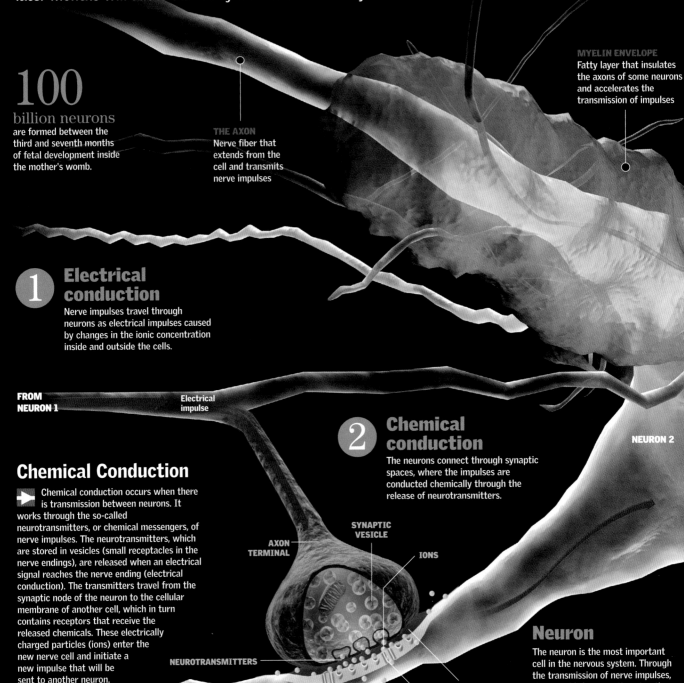

100 billion neurons
are formed between the third and seventh months of fetal development inside the mother's womb.

THE AXON
Nerve fiber that extends from the cell and transmits nerve impulses

MYELIN ENVELOPE
Fatty layer that insulates the axons of some neurons and accelerates the transmission of impulses

1 Electrical conduction
Nerve impulses travel through neurons as electrical impulses caused by changes in the ionic concentration inside and outside the cells.

FROM NEURON 1

Electrical impulse

2 Chemical conduction
The neurons connect through synaptic spaces, where the impulses are conducted chemically through the release of neurotransmitters.

NEURON 2

Chemical Conduction

Chemical conduction occurs when there is transmission between neurons. It works through the so-called neurotransmitters, or chemical messengers, of nerve impulses. The neurotransmitters, which are stored in vesicles (small receptacles in the nerve endings), are released when an electrical signal reaches the nerve ending (electrical conduction). The transmitters travel from the synaptic node of the neuron to the cellular membrane of another cell, which in turn contains receptors that receive the released chemicals. These electrically charged particles (ions) enter the new nerve cell and initiate a new impulse that will be sent to another neuron.

AXON TERMINAL

SYNAPTIC VESICLE

IONS

NEUROTRANSMITTERS

SYNAPTIC GROOVE

OPEN CHANNEL

Neuron
The neuron is the most important cell in the nervous system. Through the transmission of nerve impulses, they establish connections to other neurons to make the brain function

Formation of the Brain

Developing from folds in the neural tube, the brain finishes taking shape by the third month. Later it will develop the folds of the cortex.

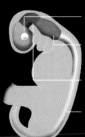

1 28 DAYS
At this stage of development, it is still possible to see the neural tube without any folds.

Forebrain

Hindbrain

Midbrain

Spinal cord

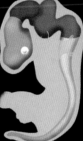

2 49 DAYS
An increase in brain size can be seen, and the general structure of the embryo begins to take shape.

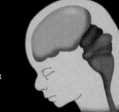

3 3RD MONTH
We now see a real fetus. The brain attains its definitive shape, but the cortex is still developing.

The Nervous System

In the third month of gestation, the fetus's developing brain changes significantly compared with previous stages. Toward the end of the month, it will have the same number of nerve cells as an adult. The nerves that run from the brain begin to be covered with myelin, a protective lipid layer that insulates the axons of some neurons to speed the transmission of impulses. The nerves and muscles begin to establish connections, setting the foundation for movement controlled by the cerebral cortex. Although the fetus can make a fist and clasp its hands, the movements are still involuntary since the nervous system is not complete.

640 miles
per hour (400 km/h)
IS THE SPEED AT WHICH MATURE CELLS OF THE NERVOUS SYSTEM TRANSMIT ELECTRICAL IMPULSES.

SYNAPTIC NODE
Axon terminal. Contains chemical substances (neurotransmitters) that transmit nerve impulses.

NEURON NUCLEUS
contains the genetic information to synthesize the necessary substances for the nerve cell.

CELL BODY
The neurotransmitters that transmit nerve impulses are synthesized here.

DENDRITES
are projections of the neuron that capture and receive the nerve impulses of the other neurons.

Electrical Conduction

The nerve impulses inside a neuron travel as electrical impulses. After an electrical impulse is generated, it travels through the axon. This conduction is produced by the exchange of calcium and potassium ions along the length of the nerve cell membrane.

NEURON 1   **NEURON 2**

Axon

First impulse

Second impulse

SYNAPSE

TO NEURON 3

3 Synaptic connection

The electrical impulse reaches the vesicles. The neurotransmitters are released into the synaptic gap and travel to the second cell. The impulse is transmitted electrically.

Boy or Girl?

B y the third month of pregnancy, the mother may be anxious to find out if the unborn baby will be a boy or a girl. Although the sex of the fetus has been determined genetically since fertilization, it still cannot be observed at this early stage of development. By the second trimester, at about 12 weeks, the fetus's genitals begin to appear but still cannot be distinguished as being male or female. The initial undifferentiated bulge has a particular shape that allows it to turn into either a penis or a clitoris. ●

Sex Is Defined

➤ Until the fifth week after fertilization, the embryonic sex organs of boys and girls are identical. Genetically, sex has already been defined, but under a microscope, the genital regions are indistinguishable. The female and male genitals are not yet differentiated. In the third month, the initial bulge that has developed has a characteristic form and is shaped in such a manner that it can turn into either a penis or a clitoris, with the usual characteristics of either. The genitals have a groove in the urethra that is distinctive. If this groove closes, then a boy is on its way. If it stays open, then the baby will be a girl. The genitals of the fetus, then, begin to grow in the fourth week, becoming visible and external in the eighth week. However, the sex will not be distinguishable until after the 12th week.

Undifferentiated
genital region

Gonad

A

Undefined

Each embryo has an undifferentiated genital system and the structures necessary to develop into either sex. The gonads are sexually undefined and have both male and female components.

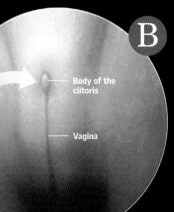

Body of the
clitoris

Vagina

B

If It Is a Girl

The vulva (which contains separate openings for the vagina and urethra) and the vagina develop from the same common structures. The clitoris will begin to form from a bulge in the urogenital sinus, the genital tubercle. The intervention of hormones is key in influencing the differential formation of each organ. The evolution might be different, but the origin is exactly the same.

THE CORD
is completely
mature and is rolled
up so that the baby
can move around
without any risk.

If It Is a Boy

By the 11th week, the genital tubercle lengthens rapidly and forms the penis. The components of what will be the genitals are progressively modified and form the elements that define the external genitalia of the male—testicles, scrotum, and penis.

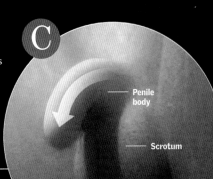

C

Penile
body

Scrotum

3.5 inches
(9 cm)

SECOND TRIMESTER
By the beginning of the
second trimester, the
fetus measures 3.5 inches
(9 cm) long.

Month
3

LENGTH: 4 inches
(10 cm)
WEIGHT: 1.6
ounces (45 g)

The Sonogram

An ultrasound image, also known as a sonogram, uses inaudible sound waves to produce images of the different structures of the body. During the examination, a small device called a transducer is pressed against the skin. It generates high-frequency sound waves that pass into the body and return as echoes as the sound waves bounces against organs, blood-vessel walls, and tissues. A special computer converts the echoes into an image.

HOW A SONOGRAM IS MADE

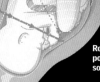

Ultrasound transducer

Reflection point of a sound wave

1 **Transmission of impulses**
The ultrasound transducer emits high-frequency sound waves.

2 **The path**
The ultrasound impulses pass through the body's tissues and bounce off surfaces.

3 **Detecting the echo**
Some impulses are reflected as echoes that the wand picks up and sends to the sonograph.

THE HEAD
is still disproportionately large in relation to the body. It represents a third of the length of the fetus's body.

THE EYES
are completely formed, although they are very far apart. They have been slowly moving toward the front of the head throughout embryonic and fetal development.

THE HANDS
already have fully developed fingers. They have fingernails and the shape of human extremities.

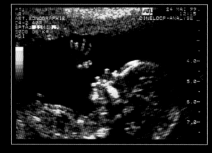

FORMING THE IMAGE
The sonograph calculates the distance from the wand to the tissues, the echo intensity, and the return time of each echo in millionths of a second. Some sonographs show three-dimensional images. They show the entire surface of the fetus and help to identify any deformation.

The Sperm

According to popular belief, to conceive a boy one must have sex on the day the woman is ovulating or the day after, since sperm with a Y chromosome (determinant of the male sex) are quicker than those that contain the X chromosome (female) and reach the egg first. If the desire is to have a girl, it is best to have sex a few days earlier: X sperm are slower, but

LIFE COMPARISON

X	72 hours
Y	48 hours

The sperm with an X chromosome are slower but have more endurance. They can last up to 72 hours. The sperm with a Y chromosome, on the other hand, are quicker but

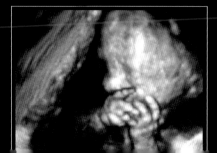

Growth Begins

During the fourth month, the mother senses the fetus's first movements. The fetal body changes; its face is completely formed. The skin has a pinkish tone, and the first ribs and cartilage appear. The external sex organs finish forming, and the internal ones differentiate. The first subtle movements of the fetus begin, although they are barely perceptible because of its small size. The fetus now occupies the entire uterine cavity and pushes the abdomen forward. Its extremities can be clearly seen. The little one enters its full growth phase. ●

Sex Development

During this period, the fetus begins to reveal the differences in its urogenital system. The undifferentiated gonad, which has male and female components that developed during the embryonic stage, is converted into ovaries in a girl or testicles in a boy. In either case, its presence will determine the development of the individual's sexual characteristics.

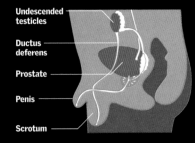

Undescended testicles
Ductus deferens
Prostate
Penis
Scrotum

Ductus deferens
Prostate
Penis
Testicles

1 MALE GONAD
Toward the seventh week, it has already been determined whether the fetus is XY (male) or XX (female). If a gonad is evolving into a testicle, the undifferentiated gonad increases in size as it descends into the scrotum.

2 DESCENT OF THE TESTICLES
At about the eighth week, the testicles leave the abdominal cavity and descend toward the scrotum. For males, the presence of the testicles and the actions of their hormones are necessary.

Amniocentesis

 is a test that is performed by studying the amniotic fluid in the sac that surrounds the fetus. After the insertion of a hollow needle into the abdominal wall of the uterus, a small amount of liquid is extracted. It is not a routine test, and it is invasive. It is done when there is suspicion of abnormalities that cannot be detected with other tests (e.g., tests for spina bifida or metabolic diseases).

COMPONENTS OF THE AMNIOTIC FLUID

98 % **water**

2 % **Organic solutes:** proteins, lipids, carbohydrates, and nonprotein hydrogenated components. **Inorganic solutes:** zinc, copper, iron, and magnesium.

Chromosomal Study

Amniocentesis gives a cytogenetic map (map of chromosomes) from which different chromosomal disorders can be detected, such as Down syndrome (an extra chromosome in pair 21) or the existence of an abnormal gene that can cause neurological or

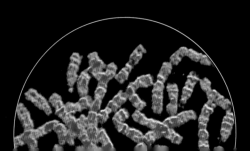

160

is the number of heartbeats per minute in the early stages of intrauterine life. Toward the end of gestation, the number drops to 120.

LOWER LIMBS
In this stage, the legs grow rapidly in a proportional manner and are longer than the arms.

BONES
can be distinguished with X-rays and have begun to change from

The Taste Buds

evelop at this stage, lthough they are ctivated only in the last rimester of gestation. The ongue has approximately 0,000 taste buds.

THE TONGUE

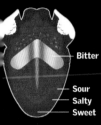

- Bitter
- Sour
- Salty
- Sweet

Month 4

LENGTH: 5.9 inches (15 cm)
WEIGHT: 5.3 ounces (150 g)

Changes in the Brain

The brain continues its growth and starts to develop folds. During most of the intrauterine period, many neuron cells are produced per second. A large portion of energy will be concentrated solely on the development of this vital organ. The areas of the brain that show the greatest growth at this stage are those that control motor skills and memory. The regions that control the basic urges such as hunger are also forming.

MOTOR CORTEX will send signals to the muscles to move the body.

PREMOTOR CORTEX will coordinate more complex movements, such as playing musical instruments.

The fetus's genetic uniqueness also starts to become evident in the development of its fingerprints.

EARS The ossicles (tiny bones) begin to harden. The fetus can sense its mother's voice and heartbeat.

The Heart

At this stage, it beats at the mother's heart rate and pumps more than 6 gallons (25 l) of blood each day. Its size is large relative to the body. The foramen ovale in the fetal heart is a hole that allows the blood to circulate from the right atrium to the left one. It will close during the first three months after birth.

- Right atrium
- Superior vena cava
- Foramen ovale
- Aorta
- Right ventricle
- Left atrium
- Left ventricle

Circulatory System

The fetus receives oxygen and nutrients from the placenta through the umbilical cord, so its circulatory system differs from that of a newborn baby. During intrauterine life, its heart is the center of a system interconnected with the lungs and liver through arterial and venous ducts that, after birth, will close and become ligaments.

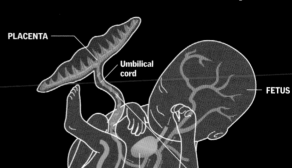

- PLACENTA
- Umbilical cord
- FETUS

THE SKIN

UPPER LIMBS

Intense Movements

The fifth month of intrauterine life reveals marked changes: the fetus's movements are more obvious and intense and are perceptible to the touch. During this period, it is important to have ultrasound exams to check for the position of the placenta, the proper circulation between the uterus and placenta, and the risk of premature birth. The future baby's features are clearly visible. ●

Energetic Movement

▶ Because of the accelerated growth and development of its internal organs, the fetus is much more active. It turns, moves from side to side, and finds ways to be more comfortable inside the uterus. It is exploring the surroundings where it lives, which makes its movements strong enough to notice. When she least expects it, the mother can receive a kick from the unborn baby. Anyone that gets close to the mother's belly can hear the fetal heartbeat through a special device.

LANUGO
is the fine hair that appears in the fifth month of gestation. It covers the entire body.

Spinal Cord

begins to develop in the fetus. The spinal cord will be the communication link between the brain and the rest of the body. The spinal cord receives and transmits information through the nerves. The nerve impulse stimulates the muscle to move.

MUSCLE MOVEMENT

1 The brain processes sensory data and sends information to the spinal cord.

2 The spinal cord receives the nerve impulse from the brain and sends a response to the muscle.

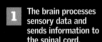

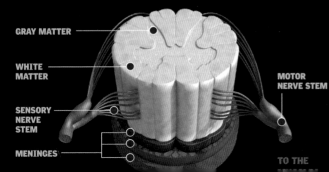

GRAY MATTER

WHITE MATTER

SENSORY NERVE STEM

MENINGES

MOTOR NERVE STEM

TO THE

Internal Organs

are in a maturing stage and most are already formed. However, the lungs and the digestive system are not yet complete. The fetus cannot maintain its body temperature or survive

5

LENGTH: 7.9 inches (20 cm)
WEIGHT: 17.6 ounces (500 g)

It is very important for the mother to have prenatal tests done periodically to monitor for possible problems or abnormalities in the fetus. Different techniques can be used to verify the fetal position and the development of its features. Sonographs produce images of the internal organs or masses for diagnostic purposes. Three-dimensional magnetic resonance imaging (MRI) allows the diagnosis of previously undetectable diseases and pathologies. In addition, it is not harmful to the fetus. 4-D ultrasound allows monitoring of the fetus in real time.

Magnetic resonance imaging allows diagnosis of the fetal position when this is difficult to accomplish with other techniques. This can be helpful in planning for the birth. Unlike conventional X-rays, magnetic resonance imaging does not have harmful effects on the fetus because it does not emit any ionizing radiation. Use of the process is recommended from the moment a fetal abnormality is suspected until birth.

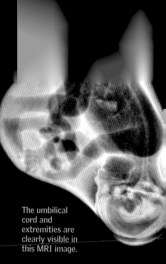

The umbilical cord and extremities are clearly visible in this MRI image.

THE HEAD is the part of the body that develops most actively. Eyes, mouth, nose, and ears are almost completely formed.

4-D Ultrasound

Incorporating the dimension of time into ultrasound exams has made it easier to observe the fetus, since the parents can see it in three dimensions and in real time while it moves. The use of 4-D ultrasound is not limited to obstetrics; it is also a tool to check the status of other organs, such as the liver, the uterus, and the ovaries.

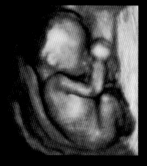

IN ACTION
The growing baby can be clearly distinguished in a three-dimensional ultrasound, which also allows fetal movement to be seen.

AMNIOTIC FLUID
The baby can swallow it and even taste the substances that float in it, because the taste buds are already developing.

Defense System

With its body and organs well formed, the fetus now enters a stage of maturation characterized by, among other things, the construction of a defense system. Fatty deposits accumulate and settle in different parts of the body, such as the neck and chest, to generate body heat and maintain the body temperature. The fetus also develops a fledgling immune system that will partially protect it from some infections.

A Song to Life

Even though the ear has not reached its peak development, it can already perceive sounds from the outside, besides those coming from the mother (heart, stomach sounds). The mother's physical state and her mood strongly influence the future baby, who can tell at all times if things are right or not.

Refinement of Hearing

During the sixth month of gestation, the ears exhibit their peak development. The fetus is sensitive to sounds outside the uterus and can hear very loud sounds. The cochlea, in the inner ear, is vital for processing sounds and already has attained its characteristic coiled shape. This is the month where the fetus prepares for life as an independent being. ●

Recognizing the Parents' Voices

With the perfection of the sense of hearing, the baby not only can hear noises and voices from outside but also can memorize them. It can recognize both the mother's and the father's voices. Since the fetus can respond to external stimuli, the parents are usually recommended to talk and play music. It can also move to the rhythm of the music and shows musical preferences. With its eardrums fully developed and fully functional, the fetus can now hear sounds originating from itself, such as its heartbeat.

Balance

The functioning of the sense of hearing is essential also for understanding the sense of balance. The inner ear has fluid that sends nerve impulses to the brain to update the information about the body's movement and to maintain balance and posture.

0.1 in (3mm)

THE SIZE OF THE STIRRUP, THE SMALLEST BONE OF THE EAR

PRIMARY AUDITORY CORTEX receives incoming sounds.

ENLARGED AREA

ASSOCIATION CORTEX interprets the sound.

SOUND WAVE PATH

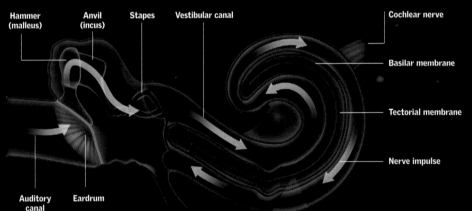

- Hammer (malleus)
- Anvil (incus)
- Stapes
- Vestibular canal
- Cochlear nerve
- Basilar membrane
- Tectorial membrane
- Nerve impulse
- Auditory canal
- Eardrum

1 Sound waves enter the outer ear canal and are transmitted to the eardrum.

2 The eardrum receives the sound waves as vibrations, which later reach the cochlea.

3 In the cochlea, the organ of Corti gathers the vibrations through hair cells.

4 Filaments in the cochlea are agitated and stimulate the nerves to send messages to the brain.

15,000

HAIR CELLS are in the organ of Corti. They convert the sound vibrations into nerve impulses, which travel to the brain to be processed as sound.

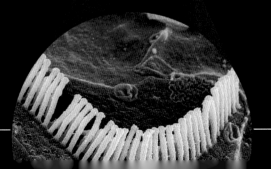

20

THE HOURS per day that the fetus sleeps. When awake, it is very active.

Month 6

LENGTH: 9.8 inches (25 cm)
WEIGHT: 2 pounds 3 ounces (1 kg)

CROSS SECTION OF THE UMBILICAL CORD

UMBILICAL ARTERY

UMBILICAL ARTERY
takes deoxygenated blood from the fetus to the placenta.

ALLANTOIC DUCT
is involved in the formation of the bladder.

UMBILICAL VEIN
transports oxygenated blood from the placenta to the fetus.

AMNIOTIC EPITHELIUM
produces amniotic fluid and speeds its circulation.

ENLARGED AREA

The Umbilical Cord

is the structure that connects the fetus to the placenta. It constitutes the immunological, nutritional, and hormonal link with the mother. It contains two arteries and a vein that regulate the exchange of nutritional substances and oxygen-rich blood between the embryo and the placenta. It is 12 to 39 inches (30-100 cm) in length, connects the fetus's navel to the placenta, and constitutes the first physical tie between the mother-to-be and the fetus. Usually there are no complications related to the umbilical cord, although there are cases where knots form that block the flow of blood. These knots can be deadly if they are not controlled or corrected.

FEET
are defined and acquire their shape. The toenails become visible.

FLAVORS
The fetus can distinguish sweet and bitter flavors; of course, it prefers sweet.

HANDS
The first lines appear on the palms. The fingers can be seen.

KICKS
The joints are already developed and the baby kicks with rapid movements.

Closer with Every Moment

The beginning of the third trimester of pregnancy marks a key point in gestation. The process of strengthening and calcification of the bones of the fetus begins. Its body needs nutrients, such as calcium, folic acid, and iron. The baby can already open and close its hands (which will soon have defined fingerprints) and also opens and closes its mouth, sticks out its tongue, and can even suck its thumb. Its skin is still very thin but has begun to turn opaque. The bones and muscles begin to have more consistency. The organs are completely formed.

Bone Calcification

The baby's bones have begun the process of strengthening through the buildup of calcium and also phosphorus. Bone growth is regulated by many hormones. As the bones are getting harder, appropriate nutrition is important in order to provide the necessary amounts of calcium, vitamin D, protein, iron, and folic acid.

300 THE NUMBER OF BONES IN A FETUS.

After birth and before reaching adulthood, the skeletal system goes through a fusion process that reduces the number of bones to 206.

PERIOSTEUM
Fine membrane that covers the bone's outer surface

BONE MARROW
Substance in the central cavities of the bones that produces red blood cells

COMPACT BONE
Heavy, dense outer layer of bone

OSTEON
A unit of the compact bone that includes layers of bony tissue

SPONGY BONE
Inner layer of bone made up of a network of trabeculae

Red Blood Cells

The production of blood cells develops in the longer calcified bones, such as the femur, in a liquid substance called bone marrow, which is found in certain bone cavities.

Month 7

LENGTH: 12 inches (30 cm)
WEIGHT: 3 pounds 5 ounces (1.5 kg)

Central Nervous System

The folds in the cerebral cortex undergo rapid development that is more noticeable toward the end of the month. The body temperature and breathing are already controlled by the central nervous system, which controls the inhalation of air.

The Fetus Opens Its Eyes

The optical structure is practically fully formed. The fetus can open and close its eyes, which will keep their sky blue color until the second week after birth, since the definitive pigmentation is attained through exposure to light. With the general development of the eyes, the fetus can already distinguish changes from light to dark. It might also be able to see its hand clearly, since it puts it into its mouth with ease.

REACTION TO LIGHT

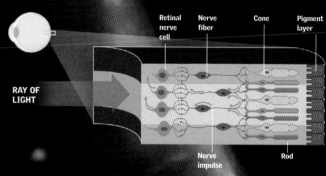

RAY OF LIGHT

Retinal nerve cell · Nerve fiber · Cone · Pigment layer

Nerve impulse · Rod

1 Light enters through the pupil and reaches the pigment layer in the retina.

2 Nerve impulse The cone and rod cells, when stimulated, transmit impulses to the fibers.

3 Reception The retinal nerve cells receive the impulse and relay the information to the brain.

Glucose Tolerance Test

In the seventh month of pregnancy, a crucial test is performed to detect the possible presence of gestational diabetes (diabetes that develops during pregnancy). In this test, called the Glucose Tolerance Test, or the O'Sullivan Test, a glucose load (about 1.8 ounces [50 g]) is administered orally to the fasting woman. An hour later, blood is drawn and the glucose level is measured.

THE SKIN
is no longer transparent and takes on a more opaque color. Layers of fat begin to accumulate under the epidermis, which makes the skin smoother.

REFLEX
The typical reflex of thumb sucking is perfectly developed by the seventh month.

Crucial Moments

The eighth month of pregnancy brings many obvious changes to the fetus. The lanugo disappears from the fetus's face, and the limbs become chubby. Birth is imminent, and before the month is finished, most fetuses assume a head-down position. The space in which the fetus has to move within the uterus is minimal, so during this time the fetus remains almost still. Except for the lungs, the organs are fully functional. That is why birth at this stage entails many risks. ●

Final Preparations

▶ At the beginning of the eighth month, the unborn baby's kicks become increasingly forceful and frequent. The shifting toward its final position begins, which in most cases is cephalic (the head toward the pelvis), although sometimes it is breech (with the buttocks toward the pelvis). If the baby is in a breech position, a cesarean section might be necessary. It is common to do ultrasound exams at this stage to verify that the baby's weight is adequate.

MECONIUM is a dark green substance that is found inside the intestine. It is the first thing excreted by the baby after birth.

2 Cephalic Presentation

In 90 percent of cases, the fetus is positioned so that the head will come out first during delivery.

1 Reduced Space

Since the fetus has reached a considerable size, it now has little room in which to move. Hence, it begins to turn and kick forcefully.

20 million

THE NUMBER OF ALVEOLI the fetus has before birth. Lung development will continue until eight years of age, and the child will end up having 300 million alveoli.

Appearance of the Pulmonary Surfactant

In the eighth month of pregnancy, a substance called surfactant appears in the alveoli. This liquid covers the alveoli, which are surrounded by blood vessels and provide the surface for gaseous exchange. The surfactant maintains equilibrium in the lungs and keeps them from completely collapsing after every breath. With the presence of proteins and lipids with hydrophobic and hydrophilic regions, water is absorbed by the former regions and air is absorbed by the latter. A baby born at eight months can have problems because it lacks surfactant.

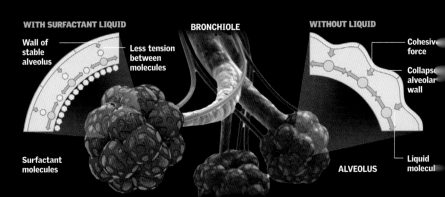

WITH SURFACTANT LIQUID

Wall of stable alveolus

Less tension between molecules

BRONCHIOLE

WITHOUT LIQUID

Cohesive force

Collapse alveolar wall

Surfactant molecules

ALVEOLUS

Liquid molecul

THE SKIN
is pink and smooth.
The fetus continues to
accumulate fat reserves
in the epidermis. The
hair that has protected
it disappears.

ADRENAL GLANDS
Located above the
kidneys, the glands that
produce adrenaline have
already attained the size
of those of a teenager.

Month 8

LENGTH: 13.8
inches (35 cm)
WEIGHT:
5 pounds 8
ounces (2.5 kg)

3 **Final Position**
The fetus has assumed its
final position before delivery.
Its buttocks will start
pressing against the mother's
diaphragm.

INTERNAL ORGANS
are completely
developed, except for
the lungs, which have
yet to be completely
coated with
surfactant.

SENSE OF TASTE
The fetus drinks
amniotic fluid and can
already distinguish
flavors with its
developing taste buds.

THE EARS
are already mature.
The fetus can perceive
low sounds better
than high ones.

EYESIGHT
The fetus begins to blink.
The iris can dilate and
contract according to the
light it receives, even
though the fetus is not yet
fully able to see.

10

THE PROPORTION OF
THE FETUS'S HORMONE
PRODUCTION compared
with an adult. After birth,
the ratio decreases.

WITH BRIGHT LIGHT

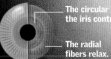

The circular fibers of
the iris contract.

The radial
fibers relax.

WITH LOW LIGHT

The circular fibers of
the iris relax.

The radial fibers
contract.

Rh Disease

When a baby's mother is Rh-negative and
the father is Rh-positive, the baby can
inherit the Rh-positive blood from the father. In
this case, there is the danger that some of the
baby's red blood cells may enter the mother's
bloodstream. Red blood cells with the Rh factor
are foreign to the mother's system, and her body
will try to eliminate them by producing
antibodies. The risk of this development
increases after the first pregnancy.

Forty Weeks of Sweet Anticipation

The pregnancy is reaching its end. During the last few months, besides the enlargement of the belly and breasts, the mother has undergone many psychological and emotional changes because of altered hormone levels. Now, a step away from birth, it is possible that she might not sleep well and may tire easily. Moreover, in this situation, certain fears and anxieties are common to every woman, so it is best to be well informed. ●

The Breasts

are made up of adipose tissue and a system of ducts that extend from the mammary glands to the outside. Along their length, they are covered by two layers of cells: an inner one (epithelial) and a discontinuous outer one (myoepithelial). At the beginning of pregnancy, the increase in the hormone progesterone triggers the enlargement of the breasts, which increase by one size in the first six weeks.

GALACTOPHOROUS DUCTS
The largest ones are in the nipple and branch out within the breast.

PHYSIOLOGICAL CHANGES
With pregnancy, they become larger and the nipple and the areola get darker, the skin on the breasts stretches, and the ducts widen.

NIPPLE
The galactophorous ducts lead here.

AREOLA
Circular region 0.5 to 1 inch (15-25 mm) in diameter. It contains sebaceous glands. Its size varies with the pregnancy.

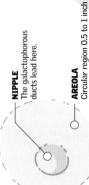

ALVEOLUS

GLAND RESERVOIR

NIPPLE DUCT

Breast-feeding

THE BABY IS NOURISHED NOT ONLY BY THE MILK BUT ALSO BY THE PHYSICAL CONTACT WITH ITS MOTHER.

MILK COMPOSITION

ELEMENTS	%
Water	87
Proteins	1.5
Casein	0.5
Fat	3.8
Carbohydrates	7.0
Other	0.2

The alveolus

is the functional unit that produces milk.

MILK-SECRETING CELL
Each cell functions as a complete unit, producing milk with all its constituents.

INTERNAL CAVITY (LUMEN)
Secreted milk is stored here.

MILK EJECTION
When the ducts contract as a response to oxytocin (let-down reflex), the milk flows inside the galactophorous, or lactiferous, ducts toward the reservoir of the mammary gland.

ARTERIAL BLOOD

VENOUS BLOOD

MYOEPITHELIAL CELLS

MILK DUCT

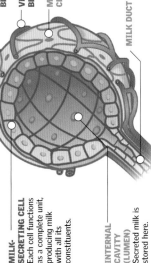

Changes per Trimester

A pregnancy lasts 40 weeks, which by convention are divided into three trimesters. Each trimester corresponds to a series of more or less specific changes that come from the fetus's different developmental stages. Many of these transformations are painful, such as the pressure of the enlarged womb against the spine. There is also an increase in weight, dizziness, mood swings, and changes in heart rate.

1 First Trimester

During the first trimester of pregnancy, the body prepares to carry the fetus. The woman's breasts grow and their conditioning for breast-feeding begins. Dizziness and nausea are frequent during this period, the cause of which is not precisely known. Also normal is an increased need to urinate due to the activity of certain hormones that generate a need to empty the bladder repeatedly. It may also be apparent that the waistline is beginning to fade.

2 Second Trimester

is the period when if first becomes noticeable that the woman is pregnant. The uterus now extends from the pubic bone to the navel, and the belly is noticeable. The heart rate is altered by changes in the circulatory system. Varicose veins can also form in the legs due to the difficulty blood has returning through the veins from the lower limbs.

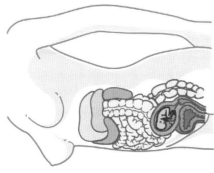

NEW LIFE
has grown from a mere embryo, and the woman's entire belly grows to accommodate this increase in size.

3 Third Trimester

The skin stretches over the belly and very soft contractions begin to be felt. The uterus has grown and pushes on the bladder, which in some cases causes incontinence. In this period, back pains become more recurrent. The large volume of the belly can often cause deformations of the spine. In some women, breathing difficulties and repeated fatigue can develop. It is also normal to develop hemorrhoids.

40%
MORE BLOOD IS PUMPED BY A PREGNANT WOMAN'S HEART.

VITAL CHANGES

1 Menstruation is interrupted
Women with regular periods (between 28 and 30 days) can notice this more easily.

2 Discomfort
Itching of the breasts, nausea, dizziness, and tiredness, even before the first month is finished

3 The uterus expands
At eight weeks, this is perceptible through a gynecological exam.

4 Movements are felt
Beginning in the fourth month, it is possible to perceive the movements of the fetus's hands and feet by ultrasound.

Childbirth, One More Step

inally, the long-awaited day has arrived—the end of gestation and the moment of delivery. Labor is said to begin with the onset of regular uterine contractions. Labor has four stages: dilation, expulsion, delivery proper, and delivery of the placenta. With each contraction, a little more of the baby's head appears, and after about 15 minutes, the rest of the body comes out by itself and the umbilical cord is cut. ●

Labor

 The labor process of birth is a joint effort between the fetus and the mother. Labor is divided into four stages: dilation, which starts with the contractions; expulsion, in which the fetus travels down the birth canal; delivery; and delivery of the placenta. Once the umbilical cord is cut, the newborn begins to breathe independently with its own respiratory system.

1 Dilation

As the mother's uterus begins to contract, the upper part of the fetus is pushed downward. The fetus begins its descent. Its first stop will be the pelvis before it reaches the birth canal.

Month
9

SIDE VIEW

AMNIOCHORIAL SAC is filled with amniotic fluid, which protects the fetus and provides it with space for movement.

LENGTH: 19.7 inches (50 cm)
WEIGHT: 6 pounds 10 ounces (3 kg)

PELVIC DIAMETER 4.3 in (11 cm)

Fetal Monitoring

During labor, the fetus's heart rate, between 120 and 160 beats per minute, is monitored. The rate decreases with each contraction and then returns to normal. If this does not happen, it could be problematic.

BPM
160
140
120
100
0

NORMAL HEART RATE

NORMAL DECELERATION

PROLONGED DECELERATION

2 First obstacle

The pelvis is the first obstacle that the fetus must face. To overcome it, the fetus adjusts its head according to the largest diameter, the oblique one, which is normally 4.3 inches (11 cm).

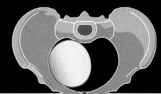

Contractions

The regular and frequent contractions of the uterus generally appear on the date of delivery. They are indispensable for childbirth to be natural and spontaneous. The uterus is a muscle, and each contraction shortens the muscle fibers of the cervix and contracts it to open it. The stage of contractions is the first phase of labor and the most important. If it proceeds normally, the baby will come out of the uterus naturally and begin its journey to the outside. Without contractions, the mother will not be able to push the baby, and it will be necessary to resort to assisted-labor techniques.

PUSHING THE FETUS

1 In preparation for delivery, the mother's uterus begins to contract at short intervals.

2 The mother's uterus contracts, putting more pressure on the upper part and pushing the fetus, which begins its descent.

3 The opening of the cervix dilates gradually with each contraction. The dilation is complete when it reaches 4 inches (10 cm).

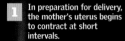
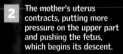
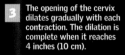
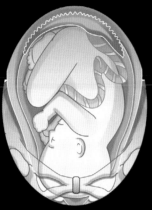

4 inches (10 cm)

THE CERVIX

The contractions of the uterus cause the gradual dilation of the cervix. It dilates completely when the opening is 4 inches (10 cm) in diameter. From this moment, labor passes to the second stage. The amniotic membranes can rupture at any time.

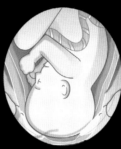

Cervix

Relaxation

After each contraction, the mother should be able to relax the uterus so that the fetus gets enough oxygen. Without relaxation, the amount of blood reaching the fetus is reduced because the uterus flattens the blood vessels as it contracts.

The Pelvis

It is important to know the shape and size of the future mother's pelvis to determine how difficult delivery will be. Any difference between the dimensions of the mother's pelvis and the unborn baby's head could obstruct normal delivery.

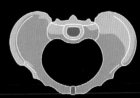

**Pelvic entrance
5.1 inches (13 cm)**

ROUND PELVIS
is the most common pelvis shape. Sometimes it may be oval-shaped. The pelvic exit usually has a diamond shape.

**Pelvic exit
4.3 inches (11 cm)**

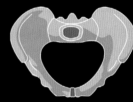

**Pelvic entrance
4.7 inches
(12 cm)**

TRIANGULAR PELVIS
In some cases, the pelvic entrance is triangular and the exit is narrower. Delivery is more complicated in these cases.

**Pelvic exit
4 inches (10 cm)**

THE SKULL
Until 18 months after birth, the skull will have cracks between its bones that will later fuse.

DIAMETER OF OPENING
inches (9 cm)

4 **Exit to the outside**
Once the head passes through the birth canal, the baby passes its shoulders, one at a time. The rest of the body comes out without difficulty. Finally the umbilical cord is cut.

Less Pain

Certain natural techniques, such as relaxation and deep breathing, can help the mother experience less pain during childbirth. In other cases, a mixture of half air, half nitrous oxide can be administered by the doctor through a mask at the beginning of each contraction. Another option is the use of epidural anesthesia to relieve pelvic pain. This anesthesia is inserted through a needle into the spinal canal. Epidural anesthesia numbs the nerves that feed the pelvis and lower abdomen. This type of injection reduces the possibility of the mother's feeling the contractions.

3 **Birth Canal**
The fetus finds that the birth canal has stretched. It rests its head on the pelvis and pushes against it. It pushes on the coccyx and is able to get its head out.

0.4 inch
(1 cm) per hour

is the rate of cervix dilation for first-time mothers. The rate increases with subsequent births.

After Childbirth

O nce the baby is born, many changes take place in the child and in the mother. After the umbilical cord is cut, the baby begins to breathe on its own, and its circulatory system is autonomous. For the mother—in pain, with breasts full of milk, and a crying baby—the situation can be stressful. At this new stage, the best thing for the brand-new mother is to rely on her intuition to understand what it is that this much-anticipated baby needs. At the same time, the presence of an involved father will favor the development of a deeper and more intense bond with the child. ●

Changes in Circulation

The fetus's circulatory system, which receives oxygen and nutrients from the placenta, is different from that of the baby after its umbilical cord is cut. The fetus's heart, which receives blood from the mother through the cord, has an oval opening called the foramen ovale. This hole, which allows blood to flow from the left atrium to the right one, closes after birth. The arterial duct, a tube that takes blood from the lungs to the aorta, also closes. The same happens with the umbilical blood vessels. When these ducts close, those that remain in the newborn's circulatory system become ligaments.

AFTER THE UMBILICAL CORD IS CUT

4 Upon the cutting of the umbilical cord, the baby stops receiving blood from the mother.

6 Blood is oxygenated in the lungs and reaches the aorta through the pulmonary veins. At the same time, the foramen ovale closes and a ligament forms in its place.

The arterial duct closes.

The foramen ovale closes.

TO THE LUNGS

FROM THE LUNGS

5 The newborn takes its first breath and fills its lungs with air for the first time. The direction of blood flow reverses.

BEFORE THE UMBILICAL CORD IS CUT

1 The oxygenated blood enters the right atrium through the umbilical cord.

2 Since the lungs are contracted, they exert pressure in the opposite direction to that of the blood and force it to change direction.

3 The blood reaches the aorta mostly through the foramen ovale and, to a lesser extent, through the arterial duct. Once in the aorta, the blood is distributed throughout the body. This brings oxygen and nourishes the fetus.

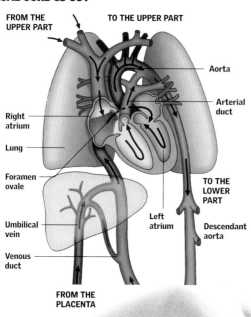

FROM THE UPPER PART

TO THE UPPER PART

Aorta

Arterial duct

Right atrium

Lung

Foramen ovale

Umbilical vein

Venous duct

Left atrium

TO THE LOWER PART

Descendant aorta

FROM THE PLACENTA

Sexual Disorders

The months after childbirth are usually traumatic for the sex life of the couple. In the beginning, sexual desire may be diminished due to the place assumed by the baby as the new center of attention. Moreover, in the first three months after childbirth, there may be vaginal dryness stemming from a lack of lubrication caused by hormonal changes. It is also normal for intercourse to be painful because of the scarring of wounds caused by the delivery. It is all a matter of time—time to readjust to the new situation, to give oneself permission to experience new sensations.

Hormonal Changes

During pregnancy, the levels of prolactin, a hormone produced in the anterior lobe of the pituitary gland (hypophysis), increase. This hormone remains at high levels while the mother breast-feeds. Prolactin is the hormone that causes milk production in the mammary glands. Another hormone released after pregnancy is oxytocin. Oxytocin brings on a reflex that causes milk to come out of the nipple. It is produced in the posterior lobe of the pituitary gland. The secretion of both prolactin and oxytocin, vital hormones in breast-feeding, is stimulated when the baby sucks on the breast. Milk production increases as the baby grows and requires more milk for feeding.

7.9 gallons (30 liters)

is the average amount of milk produced by the mother in a month. The breast milk contains lactose (a type of sugar), proteins, and fats.

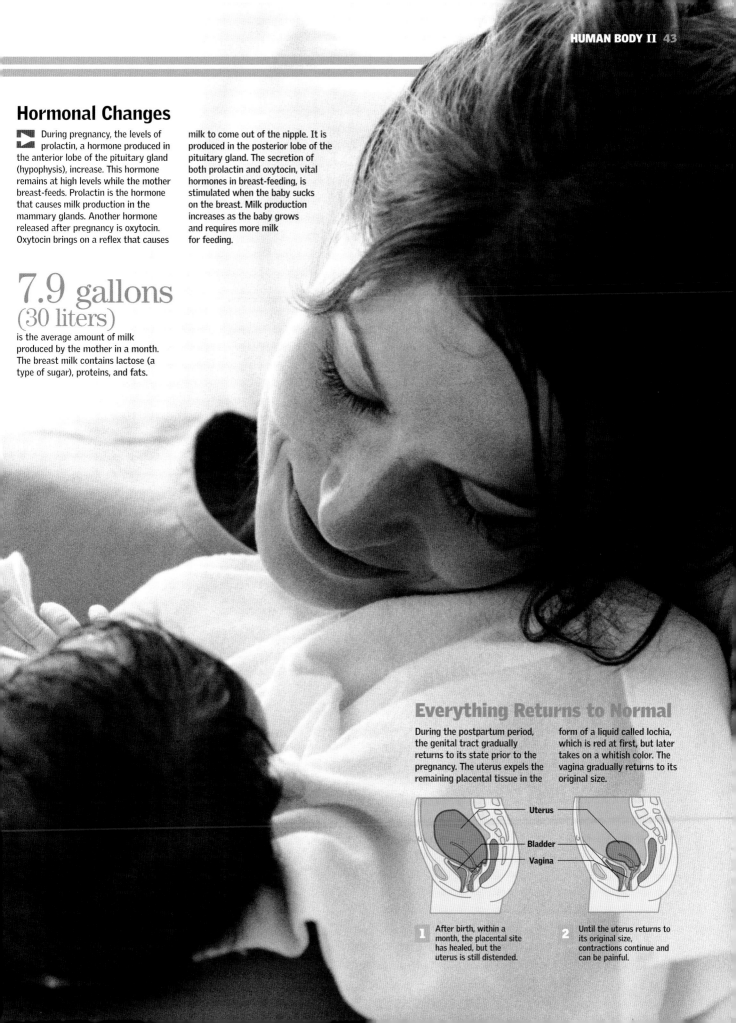

Everything Returns to Normal

During the postpartum period, the genital tract gradually returns to its state prior to the pregnancy. The uterus expels the remaining placental tissue in the form of a liquid called lochia, which is red at first, but later takes on a whitish color. The vagina gradually returns to its original size.

Uterus

Bladder

Vagina

1 After birth, within a month, the placental site has healed, but the uterus is still distended.

2 Until the uterus returns to its original size, contractions continue and can be painful.

An Answer to the Resemblance

The baby has the mother's eyes but the father's hair color; the nose is like the grandfather's, and the mouth is like the grandmother's. These and other possible combinations are caused by genetic inheritance. The genes transmitted by the father combine with genes in the mother's egg, forming a single cell that will turn into a new human being. Through cell division during the baby's growth inside the uterus, the genes will expand, and the dominant ones will impose themselves over the recessive ones. In the case of twins, the physical resemblance results because they share the same genes. ●

MODEL DNA CHAIN

DNA STRUCTURE
The DNA molecule consists of two strands that twist around one another and form a double helix. Joining the two strands are four types of nucleotide bases that face each other in a specific and complementary way and provide a cell's instructions.

GUANINE (G)

ADENINE (A)

THYMINE (T)

CYTOSINE (C)

Phosphate group

The Genes

Each human cell (except for a few, such as red blood cells) has a nucleus. Inside the nucleus are the genes, contained in the chromosomes. Each cell nucleus has 46 chromosomes with the person's genetic information. Each gene has information with a code that determines a function in the body, such as hair color. Each living being has its own genetic identification, and the genes ensure that the individual grows and functions in a certain way.

2 The Bases

face each other when the st are lined up opposite one an Adenine is always matched thymine and guanine to cytosine.

COMPLEMENTARY DNA CHAIN

INSTRUCTIONS
The sequence of the nucleotide bases (adenine, cytosine, guanine, and thymine) determines the message that will be transmitted.

Identical and Fraternal Twins

1 DNA Strands
Every strand is made of a sequence of nucleotides. Each nucleotide is composed of a phosphate group, a sugar, and a nitrogenated base.

25,000
GENES ARE CONTAINED IN
THE NUCLEUS OF EACH CELL
IN THE HUMAN BODY.

It is estimated that one in 70 childbirths produces either identical (monozygotic) or fraternal (dizygotic) twins. Identical twins have the same genes and therefore are alike and of the same sex. They come from one fertilized egg. In some cases, twins share the placenta. Fraternal twins, on the other hand, are the same in age but not in genetic material. They come from two eggs that are released at the same time and are fertilized by different sperm.

Chromosomes

 are like long, thin threads, rolled into an X-shape, that contain DNA. The genetic information is stored inside them. Their characteristic shape helps in the transmission of genes to the next generation. Each cell contains a total of 46 chromosomes arranged in 23 pairs. To form gametes, the cell divides twice, resulting in cells with 23 chromosomes instead of 46. When the sex cells join, the cell they create is a zygote, which has the 46 chromosomes necessary to form a human being.

WOMAN
The normal karyotype of women is 46XX.

MAN
The normal karyotype of men is 46XY.

 Double helix
The most common structure of DNA, a double helix, is formed from the union of two chains.

The Chromosomes

 The zygote has a cell with 46 chromosomes. As the zygote grows inside the mother's uterus, the genes go about building the baby's organs. They will determine the gender as well as the structure of the body.

23 PAIRS OF CHROMOSOMES
are classified according to their size. The largest pair is called chromosome 1, the next one chromosome 2, and so on until the last one, which is either XX or XY. In this way, the genes in each chromosome can be located and studied.

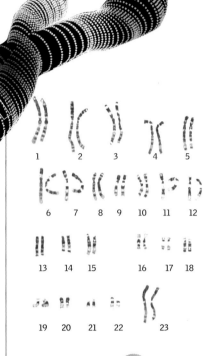

1	2	3	4	5
6	7	8	9	10	11	12
13	14	15		16	17	18
19	20	21	22		23

DNA STRUCTURE

Resemblances

If one observes different vertebrate embryos, the similarities between them are notable. These resemblances reveal that they are all descended from a common ancestor. The development of the body parts is marked by very similar genes. Morphologically all embryos possess a segmented tail, a heart with two cavities, and branchial (gill) clefts. The greatest difference appears in fish, which retain the branchial clefts. In other groups (amphibians, birds, mammals), one of the clefts transforms into the ear canal and the other into the eustachian tube. In spite of the changes in outer appearance, the observable patterns of internal organization tend to be preserved.

GENETIC DEVELOPMENT

	20 DAYS	40 DAYS	NEWBORN
BIRD			
SHEEP			
HUMAN			

Made-to-Order Babies

Genetics is also used to find out which genes a baby will have. If the mother and the father have a defective gene, they could opt for preimplantation genetic diagnosis to make sure that the baby will be born healthy. This controversial method can determine if the embryo will be a boy or a girl, and it also prevents hereditary health risks. In preimplantation, the mother takes a drug to produce eggs, which are then fertilized with a sperm from the father. Later a DNA test is done on the embryos' cells, and then two or three healthy embryos are selected and implanted in the mother's uterus.

Microlife

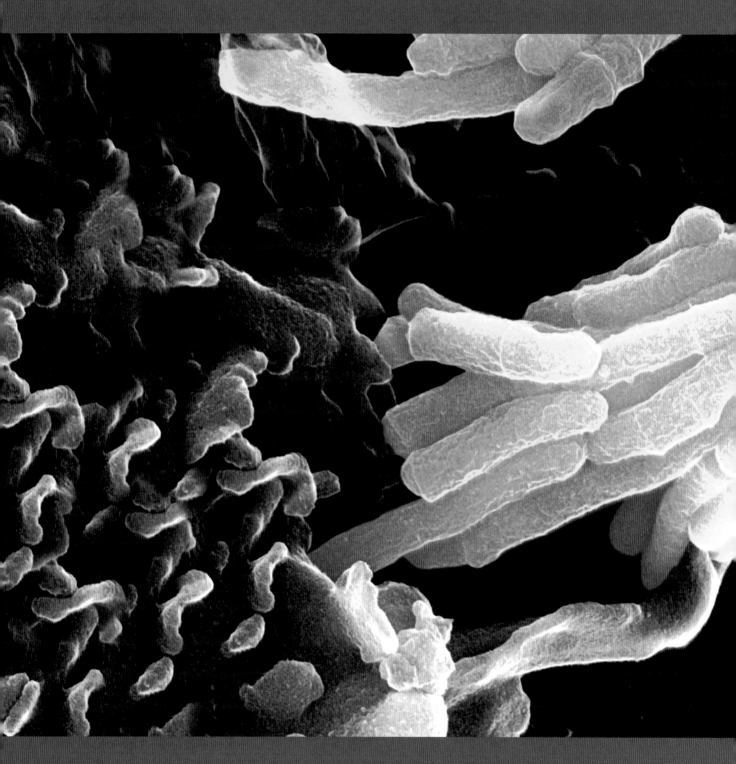

What is a bacterium? What is a virus? How do antibiotics act on them? What function do the red and white blood cells perform when they are in action? Did you know that white blood cells are bigger than the red ones and that, by changing shape, they can pass through capillary walls to reach different tissues

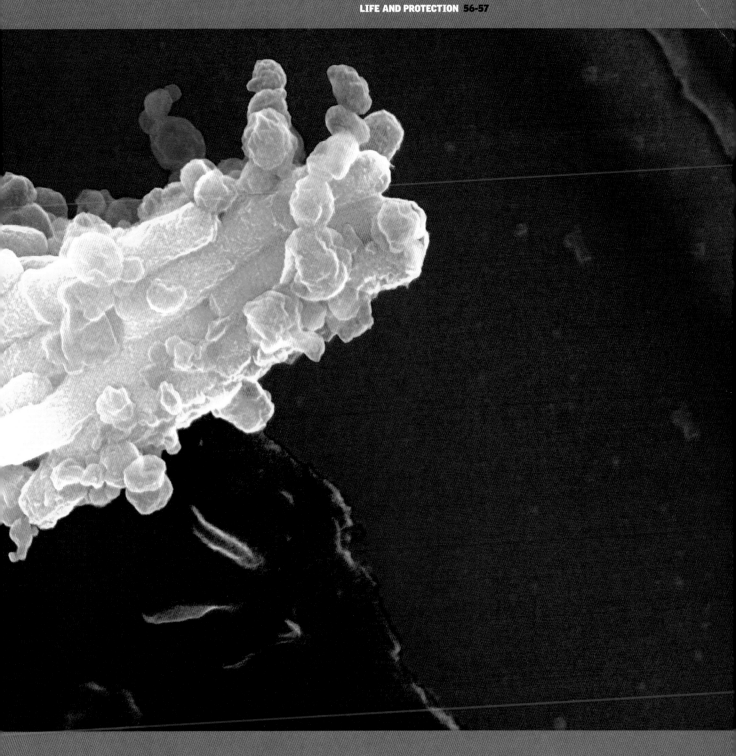

TUBERCULOSIS BACTERIA
Image of the bacteria
Mycobacterium tuberculosis (in
yellow) infecting a blood cell

and hunt down foreign organisms that are in the way, such as bacteria or cancer cells? In this chapter, we will also show you how platelets, another defense system of the body, prevent hemorrhages, or bleeding. While learning about our internal functions, you will be surprised and captivated by illustrations and much more. ●

Bacteria

Bacteria are the smallest, most abundant, and hardiest life-forms on Earth. They are so microscopic that 0.06 cubic inch (1 ml) of saliva may contain up to 40 million bacterial cells. They exist and live everywhere, from our skin to the smallest cracks in rocks. Most are benign and even vital to the survival of other living beings, but some are pathogenic and can cause diseases, some of them deadly. Almost all nourish themselves by absorbing substances from their surroundings, but some make use of the energy of the sun, and others use the chemical energy in volcanic emissions. All are made up of one cell and usually reproduce by dividing in two. ●

70% **OF ANTIBIOTICS** are produced from bacterial fermentation.

What Are Bacteria?

Bacteria have the capacity to survive in extremely hostile environments, even at temperatures of 480° F (250° C). For this reason, they are the most ancient living organisms on the planet. In a common habitat, such as the human mouth, there can be as many as 25 different species of bacilli among the 40 million bacterial cells in just 0.06 cubic inch (1 ml) of saliva. And, if there are so many in just a small amount of saliva, imagine how many there might be in the entire world —millions and millions of species. However, only 1 percent of bacteria produce diseases. Likewise, 70 percent of antibiotics are produced through bacterial fermentation.

CLASSIFICATION OF BACTERIA

Some 10,000 bacteria species have been identified, and it is estimated that there are still many left to be discovered. They are classified both by their shape and through chemical tests to help identify specific species.

A COCCUS
Spherical cocci can live isolated, and others can group into pairs, chains, or branches.

B BACILLUS
Many bacteria have this rod-shaped form.

C VIBRIO
These bacteria have the shape of a comma or boomerang.

D SPIRILLA
This class of bacteria has a corkscrew shape.

Benign

Almost all bacteria are benign and even healthy for living beings. *Lactobacillus acidophilus*, for example, is a bacterium that transforms lactose into lactic acid to produce yogurt, and it is also present in the human body in the vagina and in the intestinal tract. The bacterium *Rhizobium*, on the other hand, allows roots of legume plants to absorb nitrogen from the soil.

Harmful

Harmful bacteria are pathogenic and are present in all living beings and in agricultural products. They can transfer from food to people, from people to food, or among people or foodstuffs. In the 14th century, the *Yersinia pestis* bacterium, present in rats and fleas, caused many deaths in what was known as the plague.

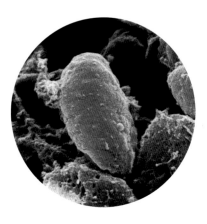

CIRCULAR CHROMOSOME
DNA molecule closed at its ends

CELL MEMBRANE
is involved in the transport of substances and contains elements that can be toxic when they come in contact with other beings.

CELL WALL
keeps the cell from exploding if it absorbs too much water. The flagella are attached to it.

Parts of a Bacterium

Bacteria are usually considered the most primitive type of cell there is, because their structure is simpler than most others. Many are immobile, but others have flagella (thin hairs that move like whips to propel the bacteria in liquid media). The cell wall is generally made up of carbohydrates, including murein, a peptidoglycan complex, lipids, and amino acids. No organelles or protoplasmic formations are found in their cytoplasm.

FIMBRIAE
are used to attach to other bacteria or the cells of other living beings.

PLASMA MEMBRANE
The laminar structure that surrounds the cytoplasm of all cells like bacteria

FLAGELLA
can be fingerlike projections.

RIBOSOMES
Organelles without membranes that produce proteins. They exist in all cells. Their function is to assemble proteins based on the genetic information from the DNA that arrives in the form of messenger RNA.

PLASMID

PLASMA MEMBRANE
Lets certain substances into the cell while impeding the entrance of others.

FLAGELLA
Bacteria use the flagella to move. Along the length of the flagellum, there is a single row of tiny hairs. The hairs provide greater support for the flagellum in water.

ANTIBIOTIC ACTION

Certain microorganisms—fungi or bacteria—produce chemical substances that are toxic for some specific bacteria; they cause their death or stop their growth or reproduction. Penicillin and streptomycin are examples. These substances are called antibiotics.

1 When a bacterium breaks through the body's barriers, the immune system recognizes it as an antigen and generates antibodies against it.

2 The leukocytes release cytokines, substances that attract more leukocytes, and by means of antibodies, they attach to the bacterium to destroy it.

3 Once the leukocytes are attached to the bacterium, they eat it.

40
MILLION
BACTERIAL CELLS
exist in only 0.06 cubic
inch (1 ml) of saliva.

WHERE THEY ENTER

Bacteria have various established pathways to the interior of the human body: the eyes and ears; the respiratory system, through the nose and mouth; the digestive system, in food and water; the genitals and anus; and the skin, the most exposed pathway, although the bacteria can enter only through wounds.

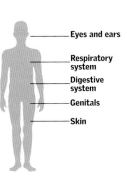

Eyes and ears

Respiratory system

Digestive system

Genitals

Skin

Minuscule Life

Viruses are not, in a strict sense, life-forms. They cannot live independently and are at the limit of inert material. They lack systems to obtain and store energy and to synthesize protein. For this reason, they are symbiotes committed to the cells, both prokaryotes and eukaryotes, on which they depend for their reproduction. Their structure might be nothing more than a simple envelope of protein that surrounds a package of nucleic acid (DNA or just RNA). In the case of bacteriophages, they invade bacteria and inoculate their own DNA into them. New viruses are produced from the copy of the genetic material.●

Anatomy of a Bacteriophage

This very small virus attacks bacteria exclusively. It has a capsid that contains the strand of DNA that is injected into the bacteria through a hollow tail body that has six fibers; these fibers allow it to attach to the cell wall.

"Filterable Viruses"

In 1898, while the origin of certain plant diseases was being studied, Dutch microbiologist Martinus Beijerinck discovered that some infections persisted even when filters for all known bacteria were used. He deduced that the responsible agents must be much smaller than bacteria. He called them "filterable virus," a word from the Latin related to "poison." They are so small that they cannot be seen with an optical microscope. Today we know that their structure does not even support the organelles of a cell: they are just chemical packages inserted in a protein coat.

ORNATE SHAPES

The shape of a virus has a close relationship to the chemical composition of its envelope. The proteins that compose it are expressed in the form of crystals, which take on geometric shapes, primarily simple and complex polyhedrons.

COMPLEX
Bacteriophage

ISOMETRIC
Tobacco

ICOSAHEDRAL
Cold

CAPSI
contains a strand of DNA that is unloaded into the interior of the bacteria when the virus attaches to i

DNA
contains all the information necessary for the virus to replicate.

FIBERS
help the virus attach to the surface of the cell that it attacks.

Invaded Bacterium

When they reach the cell wall of a bacterium, bacteriophage viruses suddenly abandon their inert appearance: they attach to the surface of the live cell and inject their DNA, which allows the virus to make copies of itself. The life of the bacteria is altered by the takeover of the viral DNA, which gives instructions to manufacture different parts of new viruses. When the attacked cell dies, its remains are used by other nearby bacteria.

① Adrift

The virus does not have locomotion. As an inert object, it is transported by water and air. When it finds a live bacterium, it becomes activated and attaches itself to the cell wall by means of six fibers on its tail.

30 minutes

is how long the virus takes to destroy a bacterium at normal room temperature.

③ DNA Is Reproduced

The bacterium has already been invaded, and the viral DNA reprograms it. The normal activity in the bacterium stops, and it begins to build the separate parts that will form new viruses (mostly viral DNA).

Attachment

Through its fibers, the virus adheres to the wall of the bacterium.

② The Attack

When the virus reaches the wall of a live cell, it releases an enzyme that begins to dissolve the wall. A small hole is thus opened in the wall of the bacterium, through which the virus directly injects its DNA.

200

copies of the virus come out of a cell attacked and destroyed by a bacteriophage.

NOTORIOUS FAMILIES

WITH RNA. These virus families do not have DNA in their genetic material.

WITH DNA. Further divided into simple-strand and double-strand viruses.

FILOVIRUSES
One is the Ebola virus, which causes a type of hemorrhagic fever.

RETROVIRUSES
The best known is HIV, which produces AIDS. The HTLV retrovirus can cause leukemia.

CORONAVIRUSES
cause diseases that range from the common cold to SARS and atypical pneumonia.

FLAVIVIRUSES
Very numerous, they cause hepatitis, West Nile fever, encephalitis, and dengue.

HEPADNAVIRUSES
Only the hepatitis B and D viruses belong to this family.

HERPESVIRUSES
The cause of chicken pox and herpes zoster, among others.

POXVIRUSES
In this group is the virus that causes smallpox.

PAPILLOMAVIRUSES
produce warts and are associated with cervical cancer.

4
Integral Production

The viral DNA that has been replicated provides instructions to the bacterium for the correct and automatic formation of the different parts of the new viruses. Once they are produced separately, the only thing left is the final assembly and proliferation of the virus copies.

CAPSID
A hollow tube with the ability to contract and inject viral DNA into a bacterium

CAPSID

FIBERS

TAIL BODY

GENETIC MATERIAL La The virus makes copies of itself by using the DNA molecule injected into the bacterium. Although the bacterium displays a normal external appearance, there are more than 100 copies of the virus being replicated inside.

5
Assembly

New capsids, tail bodies, and fibers are joined to create new bacteriophages. Once they are formed, the new viruses must wait for the break down of the bacterial wall in order to be released and attack other bacteria.

NEW VIRUS
With the tail body joined to the capsid

RECYCLING. After its cell wall disintegrates, the dead bacterium leaves remains that are taken up by neighboring bacteria.

EXTERNAL VIEW OF THE BACTERIA

6
The End of the Bacterium
The viral DNA causes the bacterium to produce a substance called lysozyme. This enzyme provokes the destruction and death of the bacterium because it digests the cell wall from the inside. When the bacterium disintegrates, the new viruses disperse. They are ready to attack again.

Fungi

ungi are living beings from the Fungi kingdom that are similar to plants, but they do not have the ability to synthesize their own food; this forces many of them to be parasites of other vegetables or animals and, of course, humans. Multicellular fungi tend to be formed by filaments and spores that reproduce very easily; others are unicellular. Infections by fungi (mycosis) tend to be superficial, such as ringworm or athlete's foot, caused by dermatophytes, but they can be systemic if, for example, they colonize the blood.

Parasitic Cells

Not all fungi cause disease. Many, which are essentially saprophytes, have a beneficial purpose. They grow on organic matter that they decompose through exoenzymes, and then they absorb and recycle it. By not being able to carry out photosynthesis, their ability to obtain energy and biosynthesis depends on the organic material they absorb.

Penicillium

This microscopic fungus, very common in the domestic environment, is used in the production of blue cheeses and is the base for the first antibiotic created by man: penicillin. Its antibiotic properties were discovered by accident.

SPORANGIA
The spherical sacs that contain the reproductive cells (spores). Because these are small and asexual, they are called conidia. As happens with all multicellular fungi of the deuteromycota type, the sporangia mature and break, releasing the conidia.

0.7 ounce (20 g)

The amount of penicillin that can be obtained for each quart (about 1 l) of culture of the *Penicillium chrysogenum* fungus with current biotechnological methods. Penicillin alters the cell wall of bacteria and destroys them.

Getting Rid of Fungi

Fungal infections respond to a variety of drug treatments. More superficial infections, such as oral candidiasis, respond to the local application of antimycotic substances. Deeper skin infections, however, particularly in persons with some sort of immune system deficiency, can be more difficult to cure. Sometimes they require prolonged administration (as long as several months) of drugs that are taken orally and act systemically (throughout the entire body). These drugs frequently have a level of toxicity that must be taken into account when evaluating the advantages and disadvantages of each treatment.

1 THE CELL
Mycotic cells, which on their own are harder to treat than bacteria, look a lot like human cells. The drugs used must be sufficiently selective to attack only these cells and not human cells.

2 THE DRUG
The main action of antimycotic drugs is to damage the envelope of the mycotic cell, which makes up 90 percent of its mass. This way, the cytoplasm is left without support and dissolves in the bloodstream.

Antifungal drug

Cellular wall

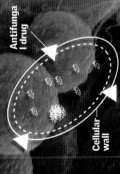

ALMOST WITHOUT DIFFERENCE
The cells that make up the different parts of a fungus are not very different from each other. Each has a polysaccharide wall that does not alter its permeability.

HYPHA
The hyphae are the filaments that make up the body of a multicellular fungus. Generally they form a networked structure (mycelium). The portion of the hypha that rises to branch off and form conidiophores is called the stalk. The fungus is the ensemble of all the hyphae and can have many stalks.

CONIDIOPHORES
The branches of the stalk that have conidia on one of their ends and which together make up the reproductive organ of the fungus.

WHERE THEY COMMONLY INVADE
Fungi are very simple organisms. In human tissues, some species generate superficial wounds (in the toenails or fingernails, skin, or mucous membranes) or even fatal infections in some internal organs.

CRYPTOCOCCOSIS
This infection can cause certain forms of meningitis (inflammation of the meninges, the membranes that cover the brain) and pneumonias (lung infections). It can also affect the skin and the bones.

ASPERGILLOSIS
Aspergillus fumigatus is a fungus that tends to spread through air-conditioning systems. It attacks the lungs of persons with a suppressed immune system.

DERMATOPHYTOSIS
This fungal infection is the most common superficial mycotic infection and can affect toenails or fingernails (onychomycosis), the feet (athlete's foot), and the scalp (ringworm). Ringworm can cause hair loss.

CANDIDIASIS
Candida species prefer mucous membranes, so they attack such areas as the mouth or vagina. Alteration of the natural flora of the vagina can lead to this type of infection, and more than half of all women have suffered from such an infection at some time.

Brain
Scalp
Mouth
Lungs
Heart
Skin
Intestines
Bladder
Penis or Vagina
Feet
Toenails

Bad Company

**0.001 INCH
(0.03 MM)**

Microorganisms can be habitual companions of the human body. There are bacteria that live in the digestive tract and interact in a positive way with humans because they exchange nutrients. However, there is a group of parasitic protists that obtain benefits from the relationship at the expense of the host's health. They are called endoparasites, and they can produce chronic diseases that, in some cases, can be deadly. ●

Sleeping Sickness

This disease in humans is caused by two subspecies of protists of the genus *Trypanosoma*: *T. brucei gambiense* and *T. brucei rhodiense*. *T. brucei gambiense* causes a chronic disease that develops over several years and is found mostly in central and western Africa. The disorder caused by the *T. brucei rhodiense* has the same syndrome but develops in weeks in countries of southern and eastern Africa. The infection in humans is caused by the bite of an insect, the tsetse fly.

MICROSCOPIC VIEW

Trypanosomes are unicellular organisms. They are characterized by their elongated shape that ends in a prominent, free flagellum. Their cytoplasm contains a nucleus and mitochondria, among other organelles.

BASAL BODY OF THE FLAGELLUM

NUCLEUS

FLAGELLUM

FREE FLAGELLUM

TRYPANOSOMA BRUCEI

Location	**Africa**
Size	**0.001 inch** (30 microns)
Disease	**Sleeping Sickness**

DISTRIBUTION

The tsetse fly, which transmits the trypanosome, is found in Africa between 15° N and 20° S. More than 60 million people are potential victims of sleeping sickness in this region.

The Tsetse Fly

Tsetse flies are representative of the genus *Glossina*. These dipterous insects are grouped into 23 species of African flies that feed on human blood; in other words, they are hematophagous. The fly's bite and saliva deposited on the human skin cause victims to scratch themselves. This opens the way for the parasites present in the fly's saliva to enter the blood.

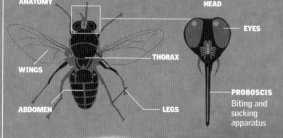

ANATOMY

HEAD

EYES

WINGS

THORAX

ABDOMEN

LEGS

PROBOSCIS
Biting and sucking apparatus

Epidemic

Sleeping sickness is limited to the African continent. It is an epidemic that affects more than 36 countries. In 1999, the World Health Organization (WHO) confirmed 40,000 cases of the sickness but estimated between 300,000 and 500,000 persons were infected with the parasite. In 2005, following increased surveillance efforts, the number of actual cases was estimated between 50,000 and 70,000.

THE DISEASE, STEP BY STEP

1

FIRST SYMPTOMS
The small wounds in the skin allow the parasite to enter into the blood.

2

SLEEPINESS
Through blood circulation, the trypanosome lodges in different organs of the human body.

3

SERIOUS ILLNESS
The endoparasite reproduces in bodily fluids, such as blood, lymph, and cerebrospinal liquid.

BLOOD
The first tissue to be invaded by the protozoan

Deadly Nightmare

▶ *Trypanosoma brucei gambiense*, the tsetse fly, and the human body are the three players in this disease. The fly sucks human blood, which already contains the parasites. The parasites undergo a series of transformations inside the body of the fly and finally lodge themselves in its salivary glands. When the fly with parasites in its saliva searches for food and bites a person, it transfers the trypanosomes. The first phase of the sickness, similar to other diseases, includes itching, fever, headaches, and joint pain. Later the endoparasite crosses the hematoencephalic barrier and attacks the central nervous system. There it disrupts vital neurological processes—including the waking and sleeping cycle—which causes drowsiness and even death.

LIFE CYCLE

FLY
bites and infects the mammal.

1 METACYCLE IN HUMANS
Upon feeding, the insect injects thousands of parasites in the metacyclic trypomastigote stage, which enter the human blood.

BINARY FISSION
New reproduction. The metacyclic trypomastigotes form.

DIVISION

DIVISION

BEGINNING
The parasite enters the mammal.

7 SALIVA
The metacyclic trypomastigotes are part of the saliva. They can be injected into the blood.

2 REPRODUCTION
The trypomastigotes multiply through binary fission.

6 MIGRATION
Procyclic trypomastigotes leave the digestive tract and migrate to the salivary glands of the fly. There they transform into epimastigotes.

MAMMALS

3 CIRCULATION
The new trypomastigotes circulate through the blood toward the different organs. The sickness can be diagnosed at this stage.

TSETSE FLY

ANOTHER FLY
bites and is infected by the infected mammal.

DIVISION

5 PROCYCLE
The parasites transform themselves in the digestive tract of the fly and divide through binary fission.

4 INVASION OF THE NERVOUS SYSTEM
The fluids present in the central nervous system are infected with trypomastigotes. The sickness already presents its characteristic syndrome.

Life and Protection

PSEUDOPODIUM
serves as a locomotive device for
certain protozoa and leukocytes.

W hite and red blood cells are the main cellular components of blood, and they play important roles in the body. The red blood cells transport oxygen from the lungs to the tissues, and they carry carbon dioxide on their return. They live for about 120 days and then die in the spleen. The white blood cells have a smaller presence than the red ones, but they are in charge of protecting against infections, and they roam the body looking for viruses and bacteria. ●

Hunter

The white blood cell detects the presence of organisms harmful to the body and traps them. The invaders are engulfed and destroyed.

White Blood Cells

These cells occur mainly in the blood and circulate through it to fight infections or foreign bodies, but they can occasionally attack the normal tissues of their own body. They are part of the human body's immune defense. For each white blood cell in the blood, there are 700 red blood cells. White blood cells, however, are larger. Unlike the red ones, they have a nucleus. By changing shape, they can go through capillary walls to reach tissues and hunt their prey.

ANATOMY OF A WHITE BLOOD CELL

In a drop of blood, there can be about 375,000 white blood cells with different shapes and functions. They are divided into two groups: the granulocytes, which have granules in the cytoplasm, and the agranulocytes, which do not and which include the lymphocytes and the monocytes. Monocytes engulf the invader, ingest it, and then digest it.

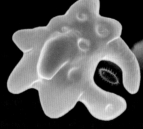
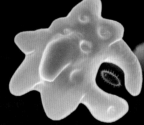

1 White blood cells can come out of blood vessels and move between the tissues. When they detect an intruder, they approach to hunt it down.

2 The cell stretches, forming a pseudopodium, or false leg, which pushes against the medium, and it then propels the rest of the cell to advance toward the bacterium.

3 It traps the bacterium and destroys it. During the fight against the infection, millions of white blood cells may die and appear as pus.

Red Blood Cells

The main carriers of oxygen to the cells and tissues of the body, red blood cells make up 99 percent of the cells in the blood. They have a biconcave shape so that they have a larger surface for oxygen exchange in the tissues. In addition, they have a flexible membrane that allows the red blood cells to go through the smallest blood vessels, obtain oxygen from the lungs, and discharge it in the tissues. The cells do not have a nucleus.

ANATOMY OF A RED BLOOD CELL

The cell has the shape of a flattened disk that is depressed in the center. This shape gives it a large surface in relation to its volume. In this way, the hemoglobin molecules that transport oxygen are never far from the cell membrane, which helps them pick up and deposit oxygen.

HEMOGLOBIN
Formed by a heme group (with iron, which will give blood its red color) and globin, a globular protein

OXYHEMOGLOBIN
Formed when the hemoglobin takes up oxygen and gives blood its colorsangre.

Platelets

These small cells are key to stopping any bleeding. They intervene in blood clotting and form a platelet plug. If a blood vessel is cut and the endothelium is affected, the platelets modify their structure and join the injured tissue to form the plug.

1
Platelets accumulate and form a plug in the wound.

2
The red blood cells close in. Together with a protein network they form the blood clot. The white blood cells fight the infection.

200,000

red blood cells are produced daily by a human being.

0.0003 inch

(7-8 MICROMETERS)

The average diameter of a red blood cell. However, the cell is flexible and can change shape.

The Most Common Diseases

Allergies are the body's response to a foreign substance, called an allergen. The most common are pollen, mites, animal dander, and nut proteins. In this chapter, we tell you which are the most common diseases that humankind suffers from today—some of them worse than others—their symptoms, and how they can be avoided.

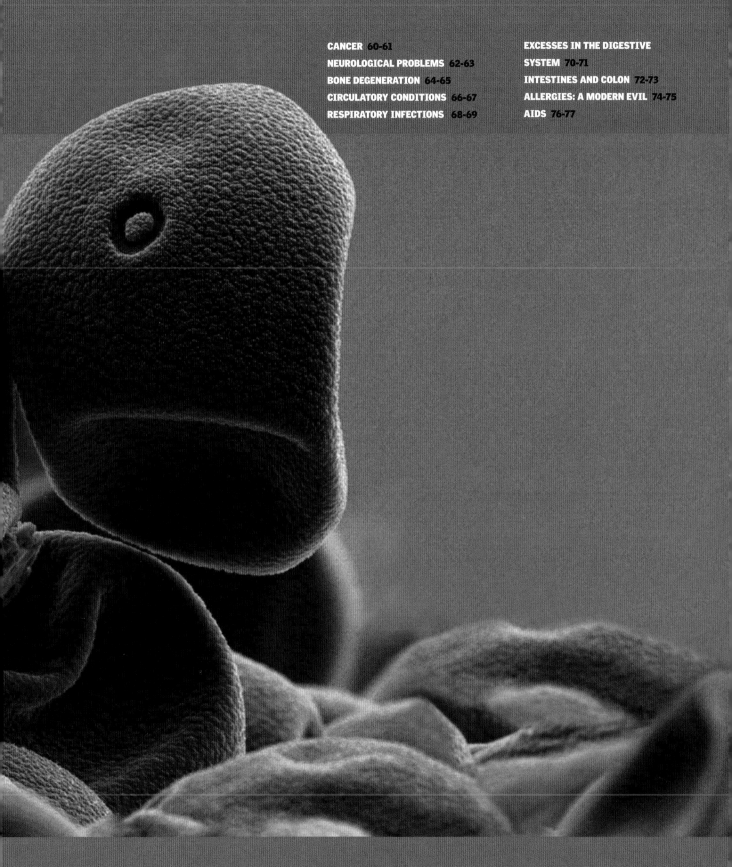

The information, written in an accessible and understandable way, is accompanied by pictures and full-color images that reveal, for example, how metastasis happens and how the AIDS virus attacks.

Turn the page and you will discover unknown and astounding aspects of human disease. ●

Cancer

he word "cancer" describes a group of more than 200 diseases caused by uncontrolled cell division. The genes of normal cells change so that regular cell death (apoptosis) does not take place, and the tissues grow much larger than normal. Some factors, such as tobacco use and excessive exposure to different types of radiation, can notably increase the chances of developing cancer. In other cases, the genes that alter the normal functions of cells can be inherited.

Common Symptoms

Although they are not always indicators of cancer, unusual bleeding, unexplained changes in weight, indigestion, and difficulty swallowing can be signs of tumors.

How It Behaves

In general, cancer consists of the abnormal growth of cells. When the cells of a tissue undergo disorderly and accelerated cell division, they can invade other, healthy tissues in the body and often destroy them. Instead of undergoing a controlled and programmed cell death (apoptosis), cancer cells continue proliferating. They can form a lump or bulge in an organ, called a tumor. Tumors are called malignant if they are formed by cancer cells; otherwise they are called benign.

Phases of Cancer

Before the definitive formation of cancer, there are two prior noncancerous stages: hyperplasia and dysplasia. The cell volume increases as the cells undergo uncontrolled cell division. The proliferation can be detected through studies done under a microscope (biopsies).

1 HYPERPLASIA
Although the cell structure remains normal, the tissue increases in size. Hyperplasia is reversible.

2 DYSPLASIA
The tissue loses its normal appearance. Like hyperplasia, this stage can be detected with microscopic tests.

3 CÁNCER
The cells grow uncontrollably and settle in one place. If they migrate and spread to other parts of the body, it is called metastasis.

Breast Cancer

One in nine women develops this disease, which causes the most deaths among women. The risk of breast cancer increases with age. The most common symptom is the appearance of a small lump in the breast, which can be removed early with surgery. Other symptoms of cancer are the appearance of blood in the nipple and dimples in the breast skin. A mammogram is usually used to detect cancer. If the results of this study are positive, then treatment can begin early.

CANCER CELLS
An agglomeration of cancer cells exhibits a protein nucleus (green) and the Golgi apparatus (pink).

Metastasis

Metastasis occurs when cancer cells pass from their original proliferation site to another that they were not in direct contact with (e.g., from the lungs to the brain). To achieve this migration, the cells build their own circulatory and feeding systems.

This allows them to penetrate the blood vessels (intravasation) and survive after extravasation. Only one in every 1,000 cells can survive the complex intermediate processes, but if metastasis does occur, it is almost irreversible and causes irreparable damage.

CHAOTIC DIVISION
Through a genetic alteration of mitosis, the cells divide rapidly and indefinitely.

METASTASIS: STEP BY STEP

1 ANGIOGENESIS
The cancer cells divide and diversify. They form their own blood vessels to receive nutrients and oxygen.

2 INTRAVASATION
After passing through the basal membrane, the metastatic cells invade the blood vessels of the body and enter the bloodstream.

3 MIGRATION
The cells travel through the bloodstream and move to a new organ, different from the one with the original tumor.

4 INTERACTION
Cancer cells interact with the lymphocytes in the bloodstream. Their adhesion to platelets leads to the formation of tumorous embolisms.

5 INVASION
Before migrating and producing the secondary tumor in a new organ, the cells adhere to the basal membrane of the blood vessels.

6 EXTRAVASATION
The cells break the membrane, and the final migration takes place. They deposit themselves in metastatic form and begin angiogenesis to arrange for a capillary system that can provide them with nutrients. From there, they begin their growth.

Primary tumor

TRANSFORMED CELL

BASAL MEMBRANE

BLOOD VESSEL

LYMPHOCYTE

Extracellular matrix

Tumor metastasis

MIGRATION
After penetrating the membrane, the cells prepare for their journey.

Most Frequent Cancers

The most common cancer is lung cancer. Because of the large smoking population, the incidence of this cancer remains high. In recent years, the frequency of lung cancer in women has increased, and it is possible that cases of lung cancer in women might surpass those of breast cancer, currently the most common type of cancer in women. In men, prostate cancer becomes more common as age increases.

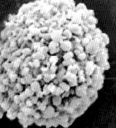

LUNG

PANCREAS

BLADDER

PROSTATE

RECTUM

BONE

BREAST

KIDNEY

COLON

OVARIES

UTERUS

SKIN

TUMORS
are produced when the cancer cells group and form agglomerates. Tumors can be benign (noncancerous) or malignant.

Neurological Problems

D iseases that directly affect the brain cause structural, biochemical, or electrical changes in the brain or the spinal cord. When some of these diseases (Alzheimer's, Parkinson's, multiple sclerosis) affect the body, different symptoms appear, such as memory and reasoning disorders, tremors, rigidity of movements, paralysis, or loss of sensation. The challenge for science is to discover a way to reverse them. So far, the symptoms can only be reduced. ●

Language

The language region of the brain also deteriorates. People who suffer from Alzheimer's tend to have trouble carrying out and expressing complex reasoning. Language disorders include lack of initiative in speaking and slowness to respond to the listener.

Memory

is progressively damaged. In the beginning, close relatives might not be recognized. Later, memory loss is complete.

Alzheimer's Disease

Alzheimer's disease, which has no cure, affects mostly persons over 60 years of age. Age and the aging process are determining factors. The cortex of the brain suffers atrophy, which is permanent because nerve cells cannot regenerate. In a brain affected by Alzheimer's, the abnormal deposit of amyloid protein forms neuritic (senile) plaques in the brain tissue. Tangles of degeneration (neurofibrillary tangles) form, which progressively damage the brain's functioning.

Neurons

Alzheimer's disease causes the appearance of senile plaques and tangles of degeneration that damage the neurons.

MICROTUBULES help transmit nerve impulses throughout the body. Alzheimer's disease causes disintegration of the microtubules.

Deterioration

As the disease progresses, the brain loses volume, and the sections of the cortex that carry out different processes are progressively damaged. The areas of the cortex shrink.

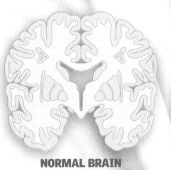

NORMAL BRAIN

1 HEALTHY CORTEX The different areas of the brain maintain their functional size. The cortex, which contains the nerve cells, is thick.

WITH ALZHEIMER'S DIS

Motor cortex

Symptoms of Alzheimer's Disease

The first manifestations of the disease are linked to the loss of ability for verbal expression. There is also a gradual loss of memory as the disease progresses. In later phases, persons with Alzheimer's can become incapable of taking care of themselves because of damage to the motor cortex.

Parkinson's Disease

Parkinson's disease is a degenerative disease that attacks one in 200 persons, mostly over 60 years of age. This neurological disorder, which affects more men than women, progressively deteriorates the central nervous system. The cause of the disease is unknown. Its appearance is related to the reduction of dopamine in certain brain structures. Among the main noticeable effects are tremors, muscle rigidity, and a slowing of body movements. Parkinson's also causes complications in speech, walking, and carrying out daily chores. Progressively tremors in the arms and legs occur, followed by facial inexpressiveness and repetition of movements.

EXPRESSIONS
Persons affected by Parkinson's disease tend to suffer from rigidity in their facial expressions.

ELECTRICAL CONDUCTION
occurs inside each neuron, preceding the interneural synapse. In Parkinson's disease, the connections and their ability to function are reduced dramatically.

DOPAMINE
Produced by the substantia nigra in the brain and transported by the nerve fibers, one function of this neurotransmitter is to influence the body's movements. The basal ganglia (deep inside the brain) receive reduced levels of dopamine. The execution of regular movements becomes altered.

SYMPTOMS
Muscle rigidity and slowing movement. Body posture is characterized by a forward bending of the head and trunk.

Multiple Sclerosis

A common neurological disorder that appears sometime between the ages of 20 and 40, it can cause distorted or double vision, paralysis of the lower limbs or one-half of the body, clumsy movements, and difficulty in walking. Multiple sclerosis occurs when the immune system damages the layers of myelin that cover nerve fibers.

MYELIN LAYER
covers the nerve fibers. In multiple sclerosis, the immune system macrophages remove sections of myelin and leave the nerve fiber uncovered, which causes nerve impulses to travel slowly or not at all.

50
percent of persons over 80 suffer from neurological diseases.

2 DIMINISHED CORTEX
The size of the neurons is reduced (atrophy). The surface of the brain cortex is reduced.

NERVE FIBER

Bone Degeneration

Because joints are made to function in very specific ways, any abnormal movement tends to cause injury. Some injuries can result from falling or being struck, while others can be caused by degeneration of the joint. The general term for inflammation of the joints is arthritis. In the bones, the loss of bone mass is called osteoporosis and is usually related to aging. ●

JOINT

BONE

STRUCTURE
The joint is normally made up of cartilage that is lubricated by the synovial fluid to allow ease of movement.

SYNOVIAL MEMBRANE

SYNOVIAL FLUID

Osteoarthritis

Osteoarthritis, the most common form of arthritis, is the process of progressive erosion of the joint cartilage. Unlike rheumatoid arthritis, which can affect other organs, osteoarthritis affects only the joints, either in a few specific joints or throughout the body. The joint degeneration of osteoarthritis could worsen due to congenital defects, infections, or obesity. Because cartilage normally erodes with age, osteoarthritis affects persons close to 60 years of age.

PHASES OF THE DISEASE

1 DETERIORATION
Osteoarthritis causes progressive damage of the cartilage. When the cartilage cells die, cracks appear on the surface of the bone. From this moment on, the synovial fluid begins to leak. Later the fluid enters the cartilage and causes it to degenerate.

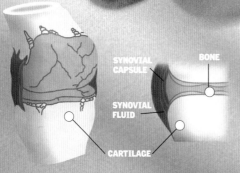

SYNOVIAL CAPSULE

BONE

SYNOVIAL FLUID

CARTILAGE

30%
or more of the mineral density of the bone is lost through the degeneration of osteoporosis.

2 BONE FRACTURE
The cartilage is worn away down to the bone and breaks its surface. From this erosion, a hole appears. New blood vessels begin to grow. To fill the gap, a plug develops that is made up of fibrocartilage.

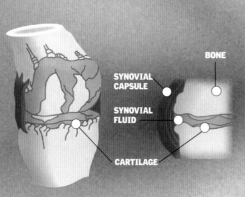

SYNOVIAL CAPSULE

SYNOVIAL FLUID

CARTILAGE

BONE

3 EXPOSED BONE
The plug disappears and leaves the bone surface exposed. If the surface fractures become deeper, the synovial fluid can enter the bone marrow and form a cyst surrounded by weakened bone. Osteophytes (bone spurs) can appear.

SYNOVIAL CAPSULE

SYNOVIAL FLUID

BON

Rheumatoid Arthritis

In this autoimmune disease, the immune system, triggered by some antigen in a predisposed person, begins to attack the body's tissues. The joints become inflamed and deformed. As rheumatoid arthritis develops over time, the tissues of the eyes, skin, heart, nerves, and lungs may be affected.

The typical symptoms are fatigue, anorexia, and muscle and joint pain.

EARLY STAGE **LATE STAGE**

Inflamed synovial membrane

Eroded joint cartilage

Synovial membrane in expansion

Symptoms of Osteoarthritis

The most common signs of the degeneration of the joint cartilage are the deformation and swelling of the joints. Some cases might include numbness and limited movement of the joint.

Gout

is caused by high levels of uric acid in the blood. The acid is deposited in the joints, causing inflammation. Primary gout is due to a congenital metabolic error, and secondary gout is caused by any other metabolic disorder.

Osteoporosis

Between the fifth and sixth decade of life, the bones tend to become more porous and to decrease in thickness. Both men and women lose bone mass, even if they are healthy. The levels of estrogen decrease rapidly in women after menopause, leading to osteoporosis in many cases. In men, the reduction in testosterone is gradual, and the likelihood of suffering from osteoporosis is lower.

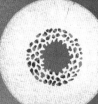

NORMAL BONE

HEALTHY BONE
An outer membrane, the periosteum, wraps around a band of hard, cortical bone and spongy bone.

WITH OSTEOPOROSIS

FRAGILE BONE
As it loses bone mass, the bone's central channel widens, and cracks appear in the osteons.

REDUCED MASS
Osteoporosis generates a decrease of total bone mass. As a consequence, pores appear that could weaken the bone.

SURFACE
is more susceptible to fracture as the bone loses rigidity because of injury to the bone cells.

PORES
appear on the bone surface as a consequence of tissue degeneration and the progressive erosion of the bone.

Circulatory Conditions

A mong the most frequent diseases that affect the circulatory system are those that result from blockages of the arteries and veins. The buildup of fat in the arteries can lead to arteriosclerosis, which blocks the supply of blood to the tissues. In many cases, as in a myocardial infarction, there are no warning signs. This could lead to the death of the tissue that loses blood supply. Certain drugs can be used to dilate blocked blood vessels. ●

Vena Cava

The superior vena cava takes the blood from the head and arms to the right atrium. The inferior vena cava takes deoxygenated blood returning from the lower trunk and limbs to the right atrium.

Aorta

The largest blood vessel in the body, with an internal diameter of 1 inch (2.5 cm). It takes blood with fresh oxygen to all parts of the body.

Arteriosclerosis

Arteriosclerosis of the cardiac blood vessels, or heart disease, is caused by a narrowing of the arteries as cholesterol, cells, and other substances accumulate in the lining of these vessels. Arterial obstruction is gradual; it begins when excess fats and cholesterol build up in the blood. These substances infiltrate the lining of the arteries to create microscopic damage sites. Atheromata form, which in turn develop into fatty masses called plaque. The appearance of these plaques thickens the arterial walls and prevents the normal flow of blood, thus reducing the blood flow.

ATHEROMATOUS PLAQUE

NARROW ARTERIAL CANAL

FIBROUS LAYER

LESION SITE

Deterioration

The progression of arteriosclerosis can be very dangerous if it is not treated. When the arteries deteriorate because of the presence of cholesterol, the organs can be deprived of the amount of blood they need to function. If the artery is completely blocked, an organ might stop receiving blood altogether and, as a consequence, completely lose its function. When this occurs in the heart, for example, an angioplasty must be done to widen the vessel once again and improve circulation in the tissue.

TO THE LUNGS

FROM THE LUNGS

1 **FREE** Without the formation of fatty plaque, the blood flows normally.

2 **WITH ATHEROMATOUS PLAQUE** Inside this plaque, cholesterol and other substances accumulate.

3 **BLOCKAGE** The arterial wall thickens and the artery is blocked.

Pulmonary Artery

branches out from the right ventricle. Each branch takes deoxygenated blood to the lungs. The pulmonary artery is the only artery that transports deoxygenated blood.

Pulmonary Hypertension

When the blood pressure in the pulmonary artery increases, the walls thicken. The blood pumped by the heart is reduced.

Pectoral Angina

Chest pains could be a warning sign that the cardiac muscle is not receiving enough blood to keep up with the demands of the work it is doing. In pectoral angina, very strong chest pains occur because of the arteries that are obstructed by arteriosclerosis.

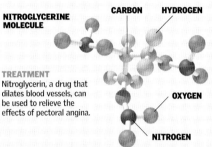

NITROGLYCERINE MOLECULE

CARBON **HYDROGEN**

OXYGEN

NITROGEN

TREATMENT
Nitroglycerin, a drug that dilates blood vessels, can be used to relieve the effects of pectoral angina.

Heart Attack

An infarction usually happens suddenly, almost without warning. The pain in the chest area can be like angina but generally is more severe and does not go away with rest. A person who suffers an attack experiences excessive sweat, weakness, and, in some cases, loss of consciousness. The attack could be a direct consequence of the lack of blood volume. If the artery begins to fill with fat after the partial obstruction of a blood vessel by a plaque, a lesion in its wall may form, resulting in the formation of a thrombus that could block the blood vessel. This could deprive a portion of the myocardium of oxygen, which would then produce a heart attack.

LESION SITE

AREA WITHOUT BLOOD CIRCULATION

LESION IN THE ISCHEMIC MUSCLE

MUSCLE FIBERS OF THE HEART

WIDENING VESSELS
To reestablish adequate blood flow, drugs such as nitroglycerin can be used. The narrow blood vessels dilate, and the heart does not have to work so hard.

1 BEFORE
The narrowed blood vessels do not provide adequate blood flow to the heart.

2 AFTER
With the drugs applied, the walls of the blood vessels relax and widen.

HOW IT HAPPENS
A blockage in a coronary artery prevents blood from reaching the muscle. If the blockage is complete, the blood-deprived muscle dies.

ATHEROMA

1 ATHEROMA
The inner wall of the artery accumulates fat, producing an atheroma.

CLOT

2 INFARCTION
A clot forms. The myocardium stops receiving blood, and this region dies.

DETECTION
When a heart attack occurs, the muscle fibers release enzymes into the bloodstream.

ENZYMES
make it possible to estimate the severity of the attack. If enzyme levels are high, it was severe.

THROMBUS IN THE ARTERY
forms when blood platelets come into contact with collagen in the lining of the artery. Fibrous filaments appear that interact with the platelets, and the clot grows. The artery becomes blocked.

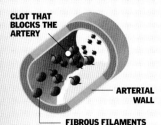

CLOT THAT BLOCKS THE ARTERY

ARTERIAL WALL

FIBROUS FILAMENTS

Thrombosis

Unlike a natural clot that forms to prevent blood loss from an injured blood vessel, in arteriosclerosis, the blood vessels are already damaged. This causes a predisposition to form a thrombus when an atheroma ruptures. In thrombosis, unlike arteriosclerosis, clots form that in many cases can migrate through the bloodstream and lodge somewhere away from the original site.

Respiratory Infections

I n many cases, respiratory-tract obstructions can cause severe complications. Although bronchitis is more often related to a viral or bacterial infection, the chronic form is associated with the consumption of tobacco, because the smoking habit has severe consequences for the respiratory system. In cases of pneumonia or complications associated with the respiratory tract, bacteria or other airborne microorganisms are usually responsible for the infection. ●

Acute Bronchitis

An inflammation of the bronchi that develops suddenly, it can result from an infection of the respiratory tract or exposure to toxins, irritants, or atmospheric pollutants. Acute bronchitis is usually caused by a virus. The common symptoms are cough, which increases the need to salivate, and in some instances a high fever. In acute bronchitis, the tissues and membranes of the bronchi become inflamed, and the air passages narrow. The amount of mucus increases, causing congestion.

HOW IT HAPPENS
The disease usually affects the large- and medium-sized bronchi. In children or older persons, the infection can expand and inflame the bronchioles and lung tissue.

1 HEALTHY
The air passage is wide enough for an adequate flow of air. The mucus does not obstruct the passage.

AIR PASSAGE

2 BRONCHITIS
The lining and tissues of the bronchi are inflamed. The air passage narrows, and mucus builds up.

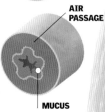
AIR PASSAGE

MUCUS

Chronic Bronchitis

The most common cause of chronic bronchitis is the irritation of the bronchi by chemical substances. The effect of tobacco, which contains nicotine, is another primary factor in the development of chronic bronchitis. The typical symptoms are cough with phlegm, hoarseness, and difficulty breathing. One effect of smoking is an excessive production of mucus, followed by enlargement of the mucous glands and dysfunction of the cilia. Thus, the respiratory tract can be affected and can even function as a medium for the growth of some bacteria. In some cases, chronic bronchitis can be brought on by recurrent episodes of acute bronchitis.

Bronchi
The lung has two main bronchi that branch out from the trachea. These two bronchi branch out further into an intricate network of bronchial branches that provide space for the passage of air in the lungs.

AORTIC ARCH

PULMONARY VEIN

Pneumonia
causes the inflammation of the smallest bronchioles and the alveolar tissue. In 1976, a bacteria was detected, *Legionella pneumophila* (pictured), that causes a severe, rapidly spreading form of pneumonia.

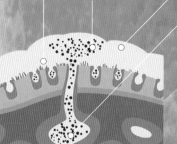
BACTERIA
EXCESSIVE MUCUS NOT EXPELLED
DAMAGED CILIA
ENLARGED MUCOUS GLAND

INFECTED BRONCHI
From the inhalation of irritant chemicals, the glands that secrete mucus become enlarged. This increases the production of mucus that cannot be eliminated from the respiratory tract. Serious breathing difficulties follow.

Cilia
are small hairs located in the bronchi. The mucus in the respiratory tract is expelled by the cilia.

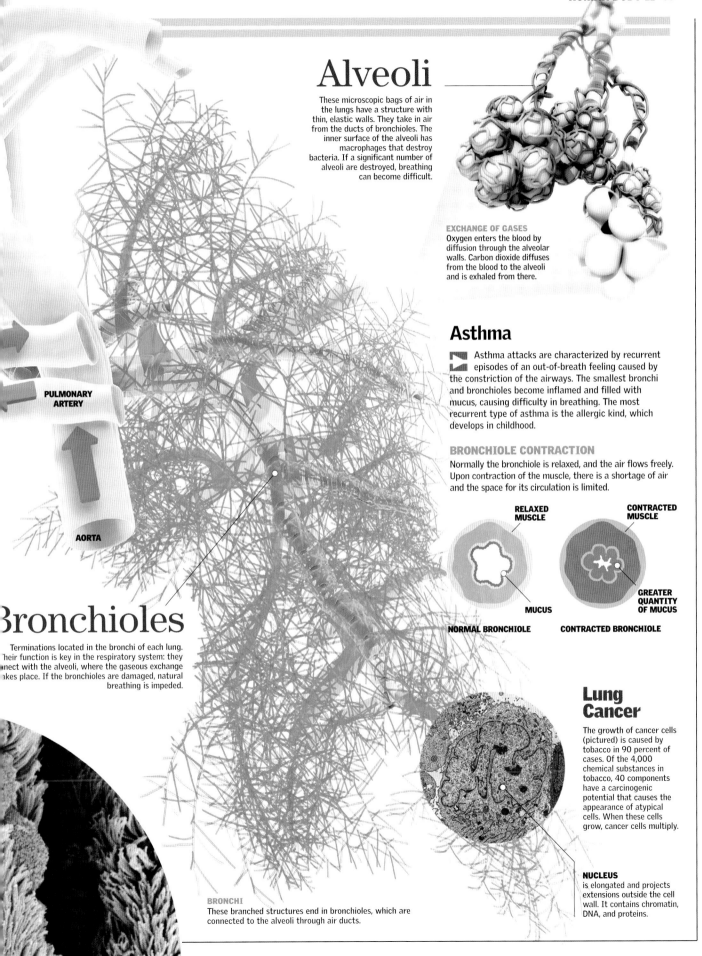

Alveoli

These microscopic bags of air in the lungs have a structure with thin, elastic walls. They take in air from the ducts of bronchioles. The inner surface of the alveoli has macrophages that destroy bacteria. If a significant number of alveoli are destroyed, breathing can become difficult.

EXCHANGE OF GASES
Oxygen enters the blood by diffusion through the alveolar walls. Carbon dioxide diffuses from the blood to the alveoli and is exhaled from there.

Asthma

Asthma attacks are characterized by recurrent episodes of an out-of-breath feeling caused by the constriction of the airways. The smallest bronchi and bronchioles become inflamed and filled with mucus, causing difficulty in breathing. The most recurrent type of asthma is the allergic kind, which develops in childhood.

BRONCHIOLE CONTRACTION
Normally the bronchiole is relaxed, and the air flows freely. Upon contraction of the muscle, there is a shortage of air and the space for its circulation is limited.

RELAXED MUSCLE

CONTRACTED MUSCLE

MUCUS

GREATER QUANTITY OF MUCUS

NORMAL BRONCHIOLE

CONTRACTED BRONCHIOLE

PULMONARY ARTERY

AORTA

Bronchioles

Terminations located in the bronchi of each lung. Their function is key in the respiratory system: they connect with the alveoli, where the gaseous exchange takes place. If the bronchioles are damaged, natural breathing is impeded.

Lung Cancer

The growth of cancer cells (pictured) is caused by tobacco in 90 percent of cases. Of the 4,000 chemical substances in tobacco, 40 components have a carcinogenic potential that causes the appearance of atypical cells. When these cells grow, cancer cells multiply.

NUCLEUS
is elongated and projects extensions outside the cell wall. It contains chromatin, DNA, and proteins.

BRONCHI
These branched structures end in bronchioles, which are connected to the alveoli through air ducts.

Excesses in the Digestive System

Diseases that affect the organs of the digestive system, such as the stomach, pancreas, and liver, find their origin in alcoholic drinks, poor nutrition, or bacteria that break down the layers of tissue and harm the organs. Diseases, such as cirrhosis, hepatitis B, gallstones, and ulcers, can lead to irreparable damage in different parts of the body. ●

Cirrhosis

This liver disease causes fibrosis and dysfunction of the liver. The main causes are chronic alcoholism and infection with the hepatitis C virus. Cirrhosis can cause a buildup of fluid in the abdomen (ascites), clotting disorders, increased blood pressure in the hepatic veins of the digestive tract, with dilation and risk of rupture, and confusion or changes in the level of consciousness (hepatic encephalopathy). Some symptoms are edema in the lower limbs, bloody vomit, jaundice (yellowish skin), generalized weakness, weight loss, and kidney disorders.

A A FATTY LIVER
can appear as a result of excessive alcohol consumption. The liver contains fat cells that infiltrate, become larger, and enlarge the liver.

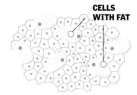

CELLS WITH FAT

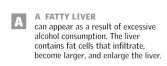

DAMAGED CELLS

B ALCOHOLIC HEPATITIS
Alcohol consumption induces enzymes to produce acetaldehyde, which generates inflammation. This damages the hepatic cells, impairing normal liver function.

C CIRRHOSIS
Bands of damaged tissue separate the cells. This stage of destruction is irreversible and can also stem from other causes, such as viral hepatitis.

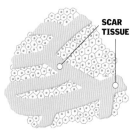

SCAR TISSUE

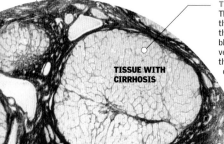

TISSUE WITH CIRRHOSIS

TISSUE
The damaged tissue affects the circulation of blood in the liver, increasing the blood pressure in the portal vein. In the lower part of the esophagus, the veins dilate and a digestive hemorrhage can occur.

Cleaning
Substances carried in the blood are modified during their passage through the liver, which cleans and purifies the blood supply, breaks down certain chemical substances, and synthesizes others.

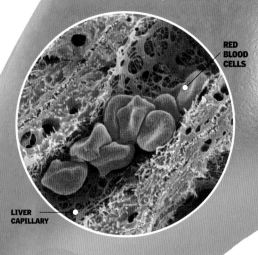

RED BLOOD CELLS

LIVER CAPILLARY

Gastritis
An inflammation of the mucous membrane of the stomach, it may have various causes, includi alcohol consumption, anti-inflammatory medication, and smoki tobacco. It is also associated with *Helicobacter pylori* bacte

Pancreas and Gallbladder

The pancreas is a gland that produces digestive enzymes and hormones. The gallbladder is a small sac full of bile (a substance produced by the liver), which it stores and releases into the duodenum (the upper portion of the small intestine) to help digest food.

GALLBLADDER
stores digestive juices produced by the liver. Sometimes they solidify and form gallstones.

STOMACH

PANCREAS
secretes pancreatic juices, which contain the enzymes necessary to digest foods, into the duodenum.

DUODENUM

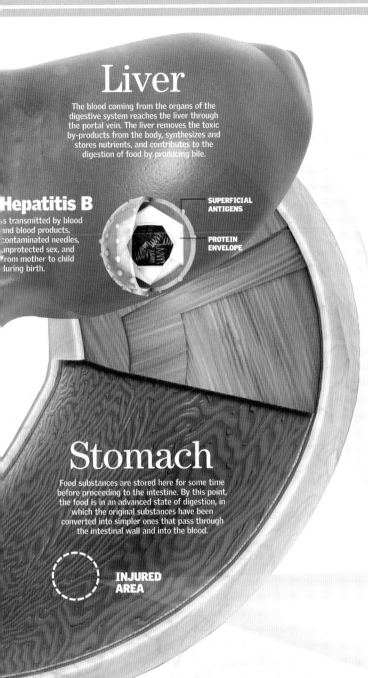

Liver

The blood coming from the organs of the digestive system reaches the liver through the portal vein. The liver removes the toxic by-products from the body, synthesizes and stores nutrients, and contributes to the digestion of food by producing bile.

Hepatitis B

is transmitted by blood and blood products, contaminated needles, unprotected sex, and from mother to child during birth.

SUPERFICIAL ANTIGENS

PROTEIN ENVELOPE

Stomach

Food substances are stored here for some time before proceeding to the intestine. By this point, the food is in an advanced state of digestion, in which the original substances have been converted into simpler ones that pass through the intestinal wall and into the blood.

INJURED AREA

Peptic Ulcer

A sore in the mucous membrane of the stomach or duodenum. Peptic ulcers are common, and one of the main causes is infection by the bacterium *Helicobacter pylori*. However, some are caused by the prolonged use of nonsteroidal anti-inflammatory agents, such as aspirin and ibuprofen.

In some instances, stomach or pancreatic tumors can cause ulcers. The relationship between ulcers and certain types of foods or stress has not been clearly demonstrated. The main symptom is abdominal pain that is more common at night, when the stomach is empty, or two to three hours after eating.

STOMACH WALL

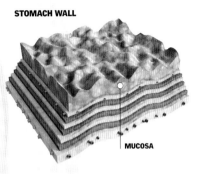

MUCOSA

1 EARLY STAGES

When the barrier of protective mucosa is altered and the stomach juices come into contact with the cells of the mucosa, erosion occurs.

ACUTE ULCER

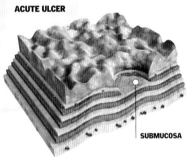

SUBMUCOSA

2 DEEPENING

The sore completely penetrates the mucosa, reaching the muscle layer of the mucosa and submucosa. An ulcer is formed.

CHRONIC ULCER

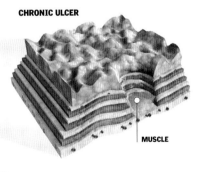

MUSCLE

3 COMPLICATIONS

As the stomach wall is more deeply eroded, a large artery could be damaged enough to cause a hemorrhage. It could also lead to peritonitis.

CYSTIC DUCT

GALLSTONES

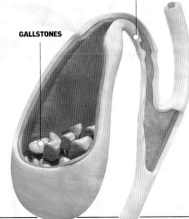

Gallstones

form inside the gallbladder, an organ that stores the bile secreted by the liver. Bile is a solution of water, salts, lecithin, cholesterol, and other substances. If the concentration of these components changes, stones may form. They can be as small as a grain of sand or can grow to about 1 inch (3 cm) in diameter depending on how long they have been forming.

1 OBSTRUCTION

The bile is blocked from leaving the gallbladder by a gallstone. This causes pain and inflammation of the gallbladder.

2 INFLAMMATION

The inflammation progresses by means of various mechanisms. The contents of the gallbladder can become infected and form pus.

3 RUPTURE

If the process continues and the inflammation is very significant, the gallbladder could rupture.

4 CONTRACTION

If the process is repeated, the gallbladder could shrink and lose its shape.

Intestines and Colon

I ntestinal infections and inflammations are among the most common disorders of the digestive system. In developing nations, an increase in infant mortality has been due to some of these diseases. Many are bacterial and can be treated with the ingestion of fluids or antibiotics, but others can be caused by a problem of the digestive system. ●

LIVER

Intestinal Infections

The most common intestinal infection is viral gastroenteritis, but it can also be caused by bacteria or protozoa. Almost all infections are transmitted by ingesting contaminated water or food. The most common symptoms are vomiting, diarrhea, and abdominal pain. Viral gastroenteritis is a self-limiting process that resolves itself in several days simply by replacing fluids to prevent dehydration, but other infections must be treated with antibiotics.

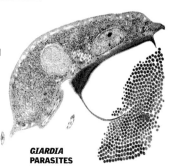
GIARDIA PARASITES

HELICOBACTER PYLORI causes gastritis and is usually found in the mucous tissue of the stomach. It can also cause ulcers in the duodenum and may be involved in causing stomach cancer.

HELICOBACTER PYLORI

ESCHERICHIA COLI These bacteria are part of the normal intestinal flora. Some strains produce a toxin that can cause diarrhea and even be deadly for a susceptible victim, such as a baby or an elderly person.

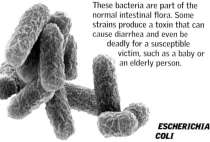
ESCHERICHIA COLI

SMALL INTESTINE

Hemorrhoids

These dilatations of veins occur in the venous plexus in the mucosa of the rectum and anus. If the affected veins are in the superior plexus, they are called internal hemorrhoids. Those of the inferior venous plexus are located below the anorectal line and are covered by the outer skin. The drainage system in the area lacks any valves.

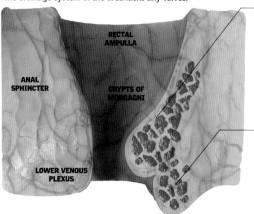
RECTAL AMPULLA
ANAL SPHINCTER
CRYPTS OF MORGAGNI
LOWER VENOUS PLEXUS

TYPES OF HEMORRHOIDS

There are two types of hemorrhoids: internal and external.

1 INTERNAL Classified according to grades. Grade I hemorrhoids are located in the submucous tissue and bleed bright red blood. Grade II hemorrhoids protrude during defecation but recede once the pushing stops. Grade III come out while defecating, and Grade IV are irreducible and are always prolapsed.

2 EXTERNAL Come from the inferior hemorrhoidal plexus. They can swell and cause pain and also become ulcerated and bleed. Thrombosis can be resolved.

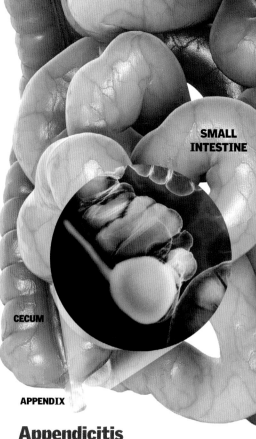
CECUM
APPENDIX

Appendicitis

The appendix is a structure that protrudes from the first section of the large intestine or colon; appendicitis is the acute inflammation of that structure. The appendix does not have a recognized function, but it can become inflamed and filled with pus. It can rupture, leading to a serious infection in the abdominal cavity (peritonitis). If this occurs, the person must get immediate medical attention.

ANUS

Stomach

GASTRIC VILLI
This image shows the walls of the duodenum where the gastric villi can be seen.

Intestinal Inflammation

Intestinal inflammations include ulcerative colitis and Crohn's disease. They can be caused by an attack of the immune system on the body's own tissues or by genetic predisposition. Symptoms include fever, blood loss, abdominal pain, and diarrhea. These conditions can be diagnosed with X-rays, a colonoscopy, or a biopsy of the intestinal tissue. The treatment might include anti-inflammatory drugs.

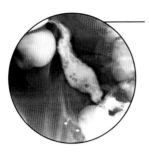

Colitis

Ulcerative colitis is an inflammatory disease of the colon and rectum. It is characterized by the inflammation and ulceration of the colon's inner wall. Typical symptoms include diarrhea (sometimes bloody) and frequent abdominal pain.

Ulcer

A peptic ulcer is a sore, or chronic erosive lesion, of the lining of the stomach or the duodenum (the first section of the small intestine). Peptic ulcers are common and can originate from a bacterial infection or in some cases from the prolonged use of anti-inflammatory drugs.

Crohn's Disease

Crohn's disease is a chronic autoimmune condition in which the individual's immune system attacks its own intestine, causing inflammation.

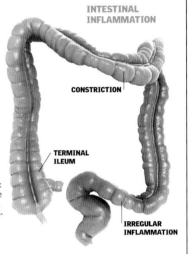

INTESTINAL INFLAMMATION

CONSTRICTION

TERMINAL ILEUM

IRREGULAR INFLAMMATION

DESCENDING COLON

COLON

Colon Cancer

This type of cancer is one of the most common in industrialized nations. Risk factors include family medical history, intestinal polyps, and advanced age. The symptoms are blood in the stool, a change in intestinal habits, and abdominal pain. People over 50 years of age should be evaluated by their doctor to check for the presence of blood in the stool (as seen in the photo), and if this test is positive a colonoscopy should be performed.

Diverticulitis

The inflammation or infection of a pouch, called a diverticulum, formed in the wall of the large intestine (colon). It is believed to be caused by the slow movement of food through the intestines, which builds up a constant pressure. This increases and pushes on the inside walls of the colon, forming pouches. Ingested food or stool becomes trapped in a pouch, leading to inflammation and infection.

1 HARD, DRY STOOL
Bulky, soft stool passes easily through the colon. But if the stool is hard and dry, the force of the contractions increases, putting more pressure on the walls of the colon.

2 DIVERTICULA
Increasing pressure against the inner intestinal lining forms pouches in weak spots of the muscle wall. These pouches can then become inflamed and distension, causing pain and distension.

COLON WALL

WEAK PARTS OF THE INTESTINAL WALLS

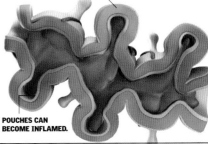

HARD, DRY STOOL

POUCHES CAN BECOME INFLAMED.

Obstruction

Cause: the obstruction of the appendix's inner opening by fecal matter or ingested foreign bodies (bones, etc.). The appendix continues secreting intestinal fluids, which causes pressure to build up inside it, until it ulcerates and finally becomes infected with bacteria.

Allergies: A Modern Evil

S neezing and watery eyes, rashes and skin irritation, swelling, and itching. These are just some of the most common symptoms of allergies, a condition that affects millions of people throughout the world, especially in developed countries. What is the cause of allergies? The immune system does not function properly: it overreacts, attacking foreign substances that normally would not cause any harm. These invaders, called allergens, might include pollen, mold, and dust mites, among many other possibilities. ●

An Attack on an Innocent

In developed countries, the percentage of the population affected by allergies has increased. One reason for this epidemic of modernity is the obsession with cleanliness. This means that the body, from infancy, is not exposed to enough dirt to train the immune system, which then reacts inappropriately to any foreign substance, no matter how harmless. Upon the first exposure to an allergen, the immune system becomes sensitized. In subsequent exposures, an allergic reaction occurs, which can range from a skin rash to various breathing problems. The reaction varies from person to person.

3 BURST
When allergens are present, the cells that help the body fight infections malfunction and respond with unnecessary chemical defenses.

2 COMBINATION
Antibodies, which are the sensors of the immune system, attach themselves to the surface of a mast cell and later bind to the allergen proteins. When there are significant numbers of antibodies, they notify the mast cell about the presence of an intruder.

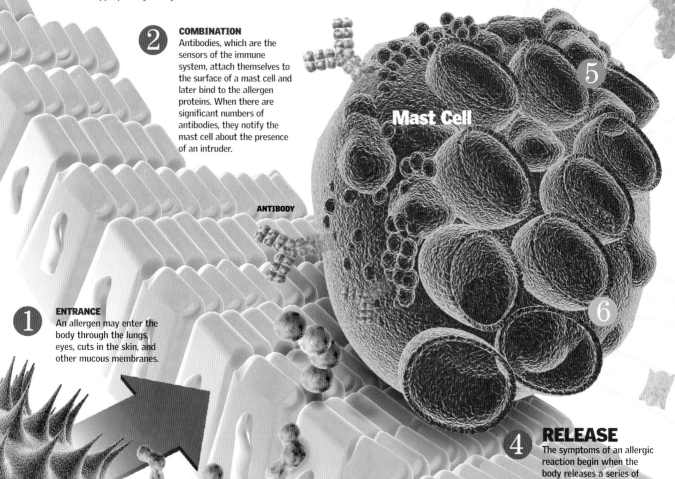

ANTIBODY

Mast Cell

5

6

1 ENTRANCE
An allergen may enter the body through the lungs, eyes, cuts in the skin, and other mucous membranes.

POLLEN
PROTEIN

POLLEN GRAIN

4 RELEASE
The symptoms of an allergic reaction begin when the body releases a series of chemical substances. Some act immediately, while others act within the first hour.

No Help from Fall

Rhinitis and asthma, like the other respiratory allergies, increase with the arrival of fall. They are incapacitating, and they exact an enormous cost in terms of lost work and school days. The cold, in turn, irritates the respiratory tract, making it more susceptible to infections, especially viral ones. Changes in the respiratory mucous membranes and the immune system activate or reactivate the allergies. A cold, for example, can trigger a bronchial asthma attack. Moreover, the lack of ambient ventilation because of the cold weather and the concentration of indoor allergens, such as mites and fungi, increase and contribute to triggering this disease.

LEUKOTRIENES

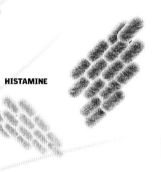

HISTAMINE

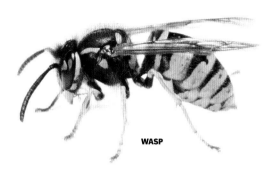

WASP

Test

The most effective way to identify the allergens responsible is through a series of pricks on the patient's arm to inoculate them with drops of allergen solutions. This test can identify the cause or causes of the illness and its treatment.

50%

⑤ FIRST RESPONSE

Prostaglandins, leukotrienes, and histamine act on the nerve endings to produce itching. They also affect blood pressure and muscle contractions, and they act on the glands to produce mucus, vasodilatation, and, later, congestion.

Asthma

This illness has grown by 50 percent in the last 10 years. Currently, it is estimated that between 100 and 150 million persons suffer from this disease, and although it is more frequent in young children, between 3 percent and 7 percent of the adult population could be affected.

Best-Known Allergens

Among all the substances that can produce an allergic reaction, these are the most important:

POLLEN: Minuscule grains released by plants during their reproductive process. They cause hay fever and breathing problems.

DUST MITES: Small insects that live inside the home. They cause allergies and asthma.

WASP STINGS: Some people have an excessive, even deadly, allergic reaction to the sting of a wasp or other insects.

PEANUTS: The allergy to this food is rapidly growing. In a few cases, it can be fatal.

RAGWEED: A type of weed that is one of the main causes of allergies in the United Sates. It produces intense rhinoconjunctivitis and, more rarely, asthma. Its pollen is very potent and is the cause of the allergic reaction.

POLLEN GRAINS

ALLERGIES BY LEVEL OF DEVELOPMENT

Developed Countries
63.21%

Developing Countries
36.78%

Allergies, like obesity, are epidemics of modernity. The more industrialized a country, the greater the affected population. In contrast, in developing regions, such as Africa and Latin America, the number of people affected is much lower. In remote regions, allergies are almost nonexistent.

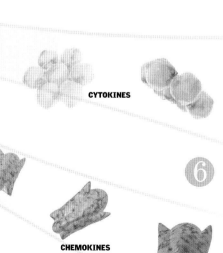

CYTOKINES

CHEMOKINES

⑥ SUBSEQUENT RESPONSES

Cytokines and chemokines, which slowly damage the tissue and recruit other cells, are strongly related to the symptoms of acute and chronic asthma.

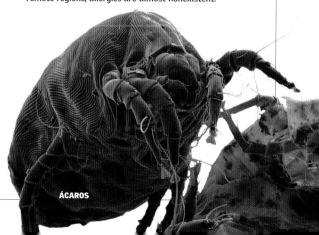

ÁCAROS

AIDS

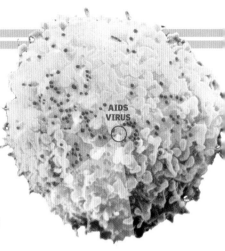

CD4-positive T Lymphocyte
Immune system cell that defends the body against infections

AIDS VIRUS

A cquired Immune Deficiency Syndrome (AIDS) is still considered one of the most important epidemics of the 21st century. Some 40 million people are infected with HIV (human immunodeficiency virus), the virus that causes AIDS; most of them are in Africa. Scientific research is aimed at finding a remedy to stop the development of the virus, but until now they have only produced therapies that slow viral activity. ●

The AIDS Virus

Human immunodeficiency virus (HIV) is the cause of AIDS. This virus destroys a type of white blood cell, the CD4 T lymphocyte, through the interaction of the viral DNA with the lymphocyte's DNA. These lymphocytes are essential to the immune system's fight against infections. For this reason, persons infected with HIV can suffer severe diseases, and even minor conditions, such as a cold, might be difficult to cure. However, not all those infected with HIV suffer from AIDS, which is the final stage of the disease. A person with HIV is seropositive. When the level of CD4-positive T lymphocytes goes below 200 cells per 1 mm^3 of blood, the disease progresses to the stage of AIDS.

History and Evolution

The "age of AIDS" began on June 5, 1981. The U.S. Centers for Disease Control found patients with pneumonia that simultaneously suffered from Kaposi sarcoma, a malignant tumor of the skin. It was noted that all the patients had a notable depletion of CD4-positive T lymphocytes. Unprotected sex and the use of needles with infected blood were the typical causes at that time. Today mother-to-child transmission and transfusions of blood and blood products play an important role.

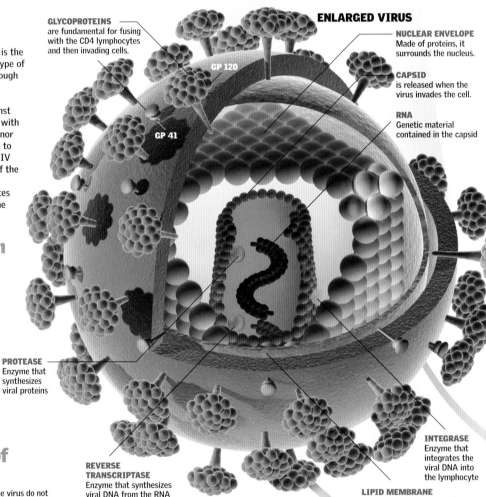

ENLARGED VIRUS

GLYCOPROTEINS are fundamental for fusing with the CD4 lymphocytes and then invading cells.

GP 120

GP 41

NUCLEAR ENVELOPE Made of proteins, it surrounds the nucleus.

CAPSID is released when the virus invades the cell.

RNA Genetic material contained in the capsid

PROTEASE Enzyme that synthesizes viral proteins

INTEGRASE Enzyme that integrates the viral DNA into the lymphocyte

REVERSE TRANSCRIPTASE Enzyme that synthesizes viral DNA from the RNA it uses as a mold

LIPID MEMBRANE makes up the virus's envelope. It houses the capsid until it is released.

Symptoms of the Disease

Many people infected with the virus do not develop symptoms for several years. In earlier stages, they might lose weight and have fever without any clear cause and in later stages have frequent diarrhea. Those severely infected are predisposed to develop various infections and cancers.

Brain If damaged, it can cause vision problems, weakness, and paralysis.
Lungs The most common disease that can be contracted is pneumonia.
Skin The appearance of Kaposi's sarcoma, brown and blue spots on the skin, is generally associated with AIDS.
Digestive system Persistent diarrhea due to an infection of the gastrointestinal tract by parasites such as *Giardia lamblia* can result.

How the AIDS Virus Works

The virus uses its layer of proteins to attach to the cell that will harbor it. A specific protein (gp120) fuses with a receptor on the CD4-positive T lymphocyte. After the immune system loses many cells, the body is left susceptible to many diseases. Ten years might pass from the time of infection until the development of full-blown AIDS.

1 **VIRAL STRUCTURE** Before attachment, the virus's envelope contains a capsid that carries the genetic material. With this material, which contains RNA, the virus will begin to act on the lymphocyte's DNA. The envelope that covers the capsid is made of protein.

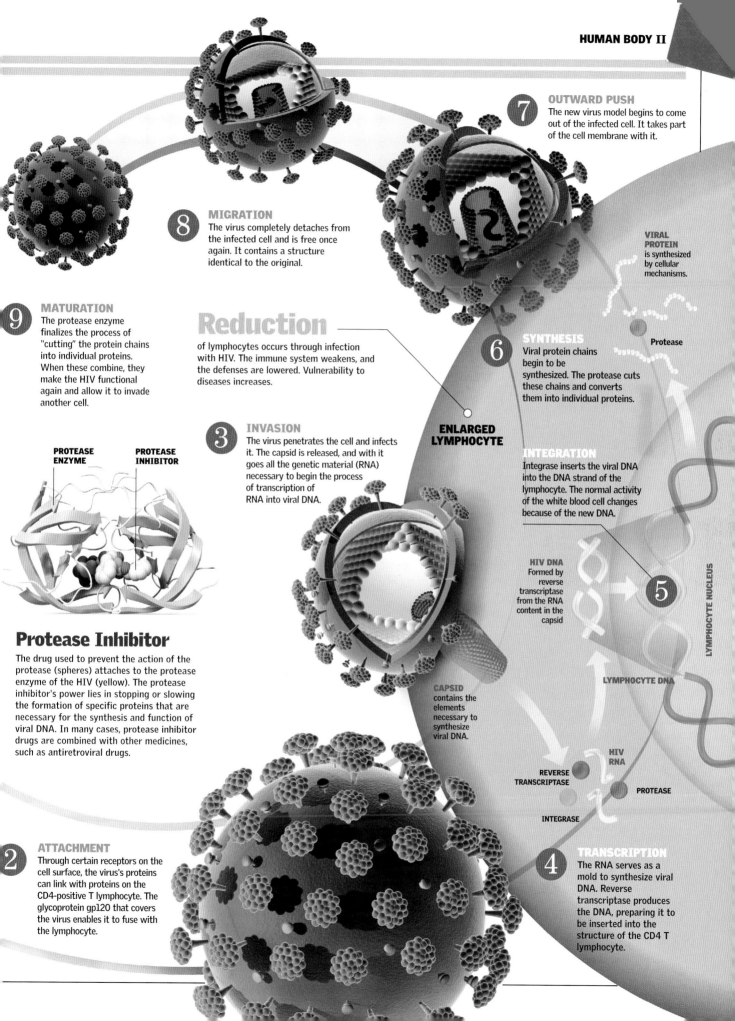

7 OUTWARD PUSH
The new virus model begins to come out of the infected cell. It takes part of the cell membrane with it.

8 MIGRATION
The virus completely detaches from the infected cell and is free once again. It contains a structure identical to the original.

VIRAL PROTEIN is synthesized by cellular mechanisms.

Protease

9 MATURATION
The protease enzyme finalizes the process of "cutting" the protein chains into individual proteins. When these combine, they make the HIV functional again and allow it to invade another cell.

Reduction
of lymphocytes occurs through infection with HIV. The immune system weakens, and the defenses are lowered. Vulnerability to diseases increases.

6 SYNTHESIS
Viral protein chains begin to be synthesized. The protease cuts these chains and converts them into individual proteins.

ENLARGED LYMPHOCYTE

3 INVASION
The virus penetrates the cell and infects it. The capsid is released, and with it goes all the genetic material (RNA) necessary to begin the process of transcription of RNA into viral DNA.

INTEGRATION
Integrase inserts the viral DNA into the DNA strand of the lymphocyte. The normal activity of the white blood cell changes because of the new DNA.

HIV DNA Formed by reverse transcriptase from the RNA content in the capsid

5

LYMPHOCYTE NUCLEUS

PROTEASE ENZYME   PROTEASE INHIBITOR

Protease Inhibitor
The drug used to prevent the action of the protease (spheres) attaches to the protease enzyme of the HIV (yellow). The protease inhibitor's power lies in stopping or slowing the formation of specific proteins that are necessary for the synthesis and function of viral DNA. In many cases, protease inhibitor drugs are combined with other medicines, such as antiretroviral drugs.

CAPSID contains the elements necessary to synthesize viral DNA.

LYMPHOCYTE DNA

HIV RNA

REVERSE TRANSCRIPTASE

PROTEASE

INTEGRASE

2 ATTACHMENT
Through certain receptors on the cell surface, the virus's proteins can link with proteins on the CD4-positive T lymphocyte. The glycoprotein gp120 that covers the virus enables it to fuse with the lymphocyte.

4 TRANSCRIPTION
The RNA serves as a mold to synthesize viral DNA. Reverse transcriptase produces the DNA, preparing it to be inserted into the structure of the CD4 T lymphocyte.

Advanced Technology

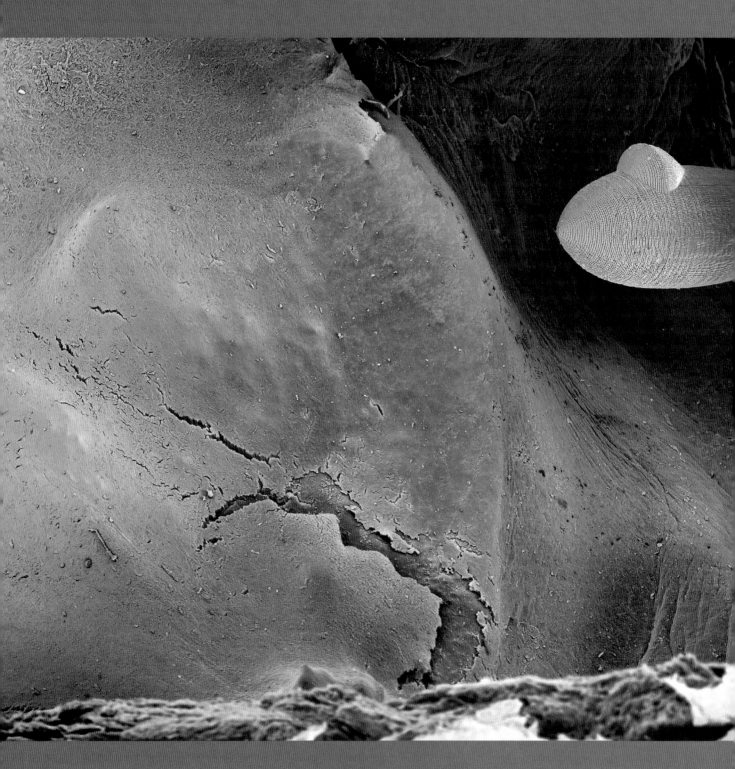

Technology, in the service of medicine, has permitted the understanding and prevention of many serious diseases thanks to the study of early diagnostic techniques, such as magnetic resonance imaging and positron emission tomography, which provide images of the interior of the body. Future decades, however, promise to bring even more

VIRTUAL REALITY
This image shows a
microscopic submarine,
small enough to travel
through an artery.

exciting developments. In this chapter, we will tell you about exciting developments like nanomedicine, whose main objective is to cure diseases from inside the body. For this purpose, devices smaller in diameter than a human hair have been developed. Among other dreams in the minds of scientists is that of preventing the degeneration of nerve cells. Enjoy the fascinating information offered in this chapter! ●

Early Diagnosis

There are various methods of examining the body to search for possible diseases. One of the most novel procedures is positron emission tomography (PET), which is able to detect the formation of a malignant tumor before it becomes visible through other methods. It is also useful for evaluating a person's response to a specific treatment and for measuring heart and brain function. ●

X-Rays

The simple emission of X-rays consists of sending out short electromagnetic waves. After passing through the body, they reach a photographic film and create shadow images. The denser structures, like bone, absorb more X-rays and appear white, whereas the softer tissues appear gray. In other cases, a fluid must be used to fill hollow structures and generate useful images. To examine the digestive tract, for example, a barium sulfate mixture must be ingested.

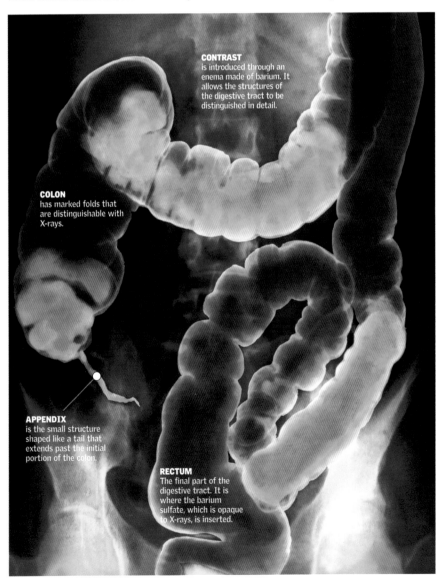

CONTRAST
is introduced through an enema made of barium. It allows the structures of the digestive tract to be distinguished in detail.

COLON
has marked folds that are distinguishable with X-rays.

APPENDIX
is the small structure shaped like a tail that extends past the initial portion of the colon.

RECTUM
The final part of the digestive tract. It is where the barium sulfate, which is opaque to X-rays, is inserted.

Scanning Methods

The different techniques for exploring the body aim to detect possible anomalies in the organs and tissues. The latest developments, such as magnetic resonance imaging and positron emission tomography, have surpassed classic X-ray methods. It is now possible to obtain detailed images of tissues and of the metabolic activity of tumor cells.

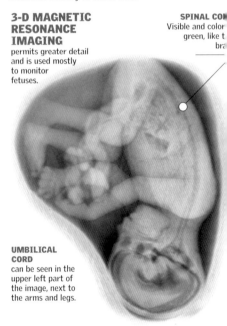

3-D MAGNETIC RESONANCE IMAGING
permits greater detail and is used mostly to monitor fetuses.

SPINAL CO
Visible and color green, like t
bra

UMBILICAL CORD
can be seen in the upper left part of the image, next to the arms and legs.

Ultrasound

A device called a transducer emits extremely high frequency sound waves. The transducer is passed back and forth over the part of the body being examined. The sound waves return to the transducer as an echo and are analyzed by a computer.

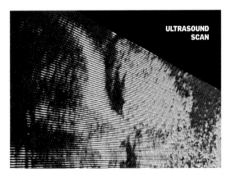

ULTRASOUND SCAN

Encapsulated Camera

A miniature camera enters the body through a capsule and takes detailed pictures of the digestive tract. It travels using the natural movements of the intestinal walls.

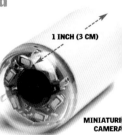

1 INCH (3 CM)

MINIATURE CAMERA

Positron Emission Tomography

This technology enables doctors to obtain detailed information about metabolic issues, such as the cell activity of a tumor. When combined with computerized tomography, it provides high-quality images and advanced knowledge regarding

diseases such as cancer. This way, it may be possible to detect an illness before it spreads.

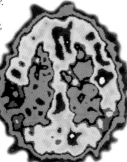

METABOLIC ACTIVITY
This scan shows the activity in a brain with Alzheimer's disease. There are few zones with high activity (red); most are low (blue-green).

HOW IT WORKS

1 INJECTION
The patient receives a dose of radioactive glucose, or FDG, which is taken up by affected organs.

2 POSITRONS
The active tumors take up large amounts of glucose. When the FDG decays, it emits positrons.

3 GAMMA RAYS
are emitted when the positrons collide with electrons and are annihilated.

4 IMAGES
A computer receives the rays and converts them into images that provide details about possible tumors.

WHEN IT IS SUITABLE TO USE
It should be used for patients with coronary or brain diseases and to detect cancer.

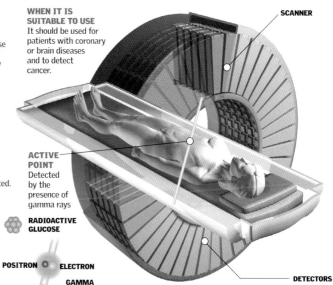

SCANNER

ACTIVE POINT
Detected by the presence of gamma rays

RADIOACTIVE GLUCOSE

POSITRON   ELECTRON

GAMMA RAYS

DETECTORS

Computerized Tomography

Computerized tomography (CT) provides information about regions denser than those typically penetrated by X-rays. The tomography covers each millimeter of the body's contour, providing many images of cross sections of the body. By

combining these images, a three-dimensional grayscale picture of a particular organ can be obtained.

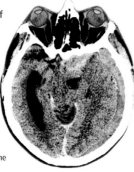

INTERNAL HEMORRHAGE
In this CT scan, a hematoma (in orange) can be seen that was formed from a blood clot after an injury to the membranes surrounding the brain.

HOW IT WORKS

1 SCAN
The patient enters the tomography machine through an opening that divides the body contour into sections.

2 X-RAY TUBE
rotates simultaneously with the detector to completely X-ray the patient.

3 RECEPTION
The detectors sense the intensity of the rays as they pass over each point of the body.

4 IMAGE
The information is processed by a computer that integrates the data into images.

WHEN IT IS SUITABLE TO USE
It should be used when images of internal organs of the body are needed.

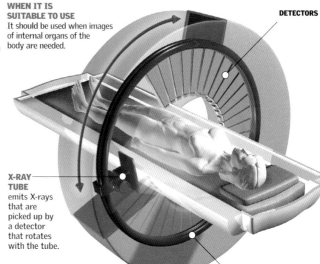

DETECTORS

X-RAY TUBE
emits X-rays that are picked up by a detector that rotates with the tube.

TOMOGRAPHY

Magnetic Resonance Imaging

A technique that uses a cylindrical chamber capable of producing a magnetic field 40,000 times stronger than the earth's. Unlike X-rays, magnetic resonance allows imaging of soft tissues (like fat) and from every angle. It provides the

most detailed images and is used most frequently for examining the brain.

BRAIN
The fibers of the nerve cells that transmit electrical signals are shown in color.

HOW IT WORKS

1 MAGNETIC FIELD
acts on the hydrogen atoms of the body when the patient enters the magnetized chamber.

2 RADIO WAVES
are applied to the hydrogen atoms. Upon receiving these waves, they emit a corresponding radio wave.

3 PROCESSING
A computer receives and processes the signals emitted by the atoms and then builds an image from them.

WHEN IT IS SUITABLE TO USE
It should be used when the anatomy of the softest tissues, which X-rays cannot reveal, need to be examined.

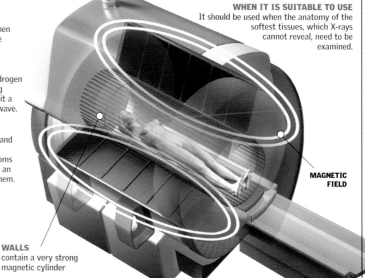

MAGNETIC FIELD

WALLS
contain a very strong magnetic cylinder

Laser Surgery

Surgeries performed with laser beam techniques are much simpler than traditional procedures. Lasers are frequently used in eye surgery. They can close blood vessels in the retina. Lasers can also burn papillomas (benign epithelial tumors) and excise precancerous lesions from the mouth without scarring. Currently lasers are used to break down kidney stones and to open clogged arteries. ●

Laser Angioplasty

When fatty deposits (atheromas) accumulate in the arteries, plaque forms, and the internal channel for blood flow narrows. Laser angioplasty can be used to eliminate this plaque. In this operation, a catheter with a small balloon is used. The balloon is introduced into the artery and is inflated to momentarily cut off the circulation. The plaque is removed easily by a laser emitter located at the tip of the catheter. The laser angioplasty operation is quick, and the patient's recovery period is usually short. Laser angioplasty is recommended when only one artery is blocked.

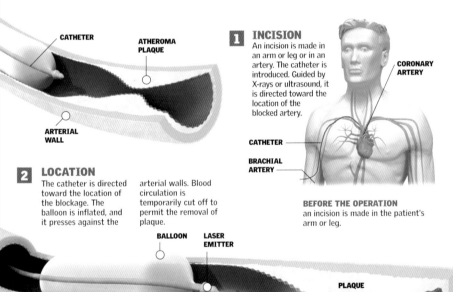

CATHETER

ATHEROMA PLAQUE

ARTERIAL WALL

2 LOCATION
The catheter is directed toward the location of the blockage. The balloon is inflated, and it presses against the arterial walls. Blood circulation is temporarily cut off to permit the removal of plaque.

BALLOON

LASER EMITTER

PLAQUE

PLAQUE

3 DESTRUCTION
From the tip of the catheter, the laser emitter applies a beam directly on the atheromas of the artery. The fragments of plaque are removed through a vacuum mechanism.

WIDENED ARTERIAL CHANNEL

1 INCISION
An incision is made in an arm or leg or in an artery. The catheter is introduced. Guided by X-rays or ultrasound, it is directed toward the location of the blocked artery.

CORONARY ARTERY

CATHETER

BRACHIAL ARTERY

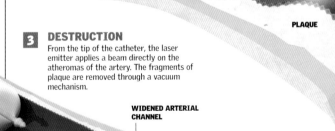

BEFORE THE OPERATION
an incision is made in the patient's arm or leg.

4 CONTROL
Once the process of destroying the plaque is finished, the blood pressure is checked on both sides of the arterial wall to ensure that it is equal. The catheter with the balloon is then removed. The recovery period is short; the patient only needs a brief postoperative rest period.

Pupil Contraction

The pupil plays an important role in regulating the light that enters the eye. In a normally functioning eye, light enters through the pupil, passes through the cornea and the lens, and finally reaches the retina. When the ambient light is intense, the pupil contracts. This causes the eye to receive less light and prevents glare. The contraction of the pupil is a reflex action.

CONTRACTED PUPIL

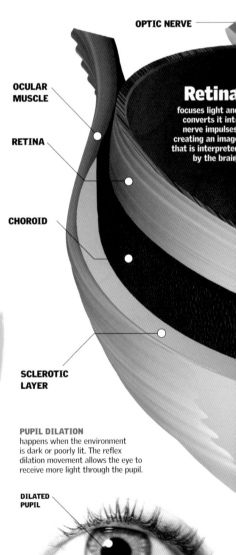

OPTIC NERVE

OCULAR MUSCLE

RETINA

CHOROID

Retina
focuses light and converts it into nerve impulses creating an image that is interpreted by the brain

SCLEROTIC LAYER

PUPIL DILATION
happens when the environment is dark or poorly lit. The reflex dilation movement allows the eye to receive more light through the pupil.

DILATED PUPIL

OCULAR MUSCLE

RETINA

NORMAL VISION

The eye works like a photographic camera. Light reaches the pupil and is refracted by the cornea. Behind it, a lens adjusts its structure automatically to focus the light rays onto the retina, creating an inverted image of the viewed object. Nerve cells in the retina transform the image into nerve impulses that reach the brain. The brain then interprets the information and corrects the image.

FOCUSING occurs on the retina.

CORNEA

PUPIL

LENS

LASIK Surgery

The procedure is very simple and takes only 15 minutes. The cornea is shaped so that images will be more precisely focused on the retina. The cornea's structure is modified depending on the condition being corrected (such as astigmatism or myopia).

1 **LOCAL ANESTHETIC**
An anesthetic is applied to the eye in the form of drops to allow the eye to remain open.

2 **EXTERNAL LAMELLA**
A small cut is made on the cornea. A very thin flap is lifted where the laser beam will enter.

3 **LASER BEAM**
In only five minutes, the center of the cornea is shaped by the laser beam, which is controlled by a computer. The cornea is made:

FLATTER
for cases of myopia

OR MORE CURVED
for cases of astigmatism.

Lens

focuses the light rays before they reach the retina, a process necessary for both near and far vision.

IRIS

LENS

0.2 INCH (5 MM)

CORNEA

A BIT OF HISTORY

12,000 years ago, convex pieces of glass were used to magnify objects. Laser techniques have revolutionized the correction of visual problems.

2283 BC
Official writings from the Chinese empire note that lenses were used to observe the sky.

AD 1290
Two pieces of Murano (Venetian) glass were joined by wooden or shell rims. In the Middle Ages, wearing glasses was considered a sign of wisdom.

1887
Adolf Fick built the first prototype for contact lenses made out of glass. They were placed over the sclera of the eye.

4 **FINAL STEP**
The flap is returned to its original location. It adheres to the cornea without the need for stitches. The patient is able to walk out of the operating room.

PUPIL

ULTRAVIOLET RAY

1971
The first contact lenses for daily use appeared. Fifteen years later, disposable contact lenses would appear.

LASER BEAM
An intense ray of light that has only one wavelength, such as ultraviolet or infrared. Lasers were discovered in 1960 and have diverse applications.

1995
The LASIK technique was developed. A laser beam corrects the cornea in a 15-minute operation.

EYELID

Transplants

When the possibilities for treating certain diseases run out, the only remaining alternative is to replace the sick organ with another one through a transplant. The organs can come from a live person (as long as it does not cause harm to that person, as in the case of kidney donation) or from a donor corpse. Today the most novel transplant is the face transplant, which involves working with many nerves and is highly complex. ●

Organ Transplants

Of the two types of transplant operations (organs and tissues), organ transplants are by far the more difficult. They require complex surgeries to achieve the splicing of vessel and ducts. Tissue transplants are simpler: cells are injected, to b implanted later.

TYPES OF TRANSPLANTS

Allograft: Consists of the donation of organs from one individual to another genetically different individual of the same species.

Autograft: A transplant in which the donor and the recipient are the same person. The typical case is a skin graft from a healthy site to an injured one.

Isograft: A transplant in which the donor and the recipient are genetically identical.

Xenograft: A transplant in which the donor and the recipient ar of different species (e.g., from a monkey to a human). This type generates the strongest rejection response by the body of the recipient.

The Mouth and Nose of Another Person

The operation for replacing the damaged face (generally due to burns) is still in its developing stage. The first recorded case of a successful transplant was that of Isabelle Dinoire, a French woman who lost her nose, her chin, and her lips when she was savagely attacked by her dog in 2005. The surgery was partial, and it restored those parts she had lost with skin donated by a sick woman suffering a case of cerebral coma. The complex operation included the ligation of blood vessels and nerves between the donating tissue and the beneficiary.

The nerves can only be joined through microsurgery. The operation is very complicated because the face is full of nerve endings.

SUBCUTANEOUS FAT

ORBICULAR MUSCLE OF THE EYE

SKIN

TEMPORAL MUSCLE

ZYGOMATICUS MAJOR MUSCLE

ORBICULAR MUSCLE OF THE MOUTH

MASSETER MUSCLE

RISORIUS MUSCLE

MENTALIS MUSCLE

DEPRESSOR MUSCLE

REMOVAL
The skin of the patient's face is removed. A wide range of injuries can be treated with this surgery. The transplant can be partial or total. In France, a woman attacked by a dog lost her nose, lips, and chin and underwent a partial face transplant to recover these parts.

1

PREPARATION
Since the face is a complex framework of blood vessels, capillaries, arteries, and veins, care must be taken during the insertion of the new face. The original muscles and nerves are left on the patient. Blood vessels are cut before the surgery. Later they will be joined to the donated skin.

2

ALIGNMENT
The surgeons position the donated skin, aligning it exactly over the face of the patient. Through microsurgery, the blood vessels and nerves are connected to the new tissue. As the blood begins to circulate, the face takes on a progressively pinker color, characteristic of tissue with normal blood supply.

3

RESTORATION
The skin is sutured, as shown in the image. The areas should normalize within 14 days. After the surgery, the patient usually requires psychological treatment to better cope with the idea that he or she now possesses a "hybrid" face, with his or her own bone structure, but the skin and fatty tissues of someone else.

4

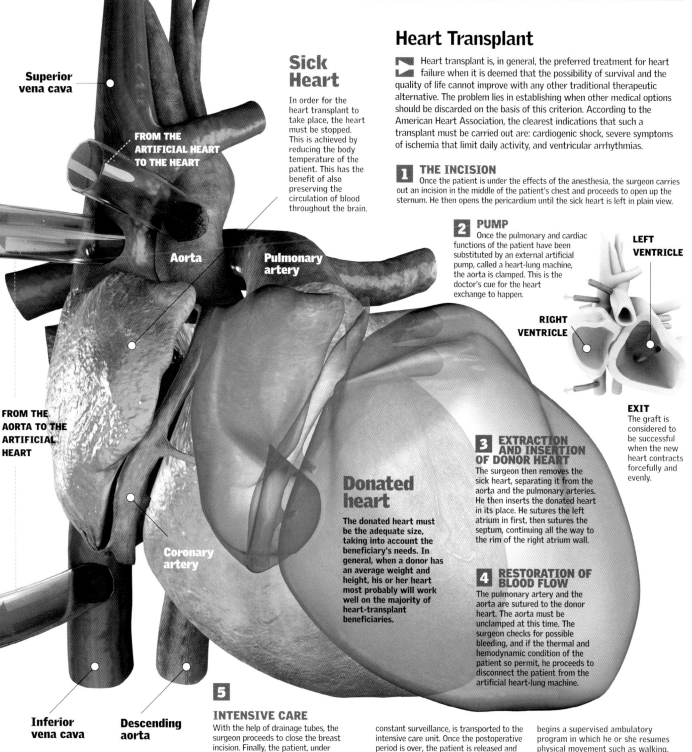

Superior vena cava

FROM THE ARTIFICIAL HEART TO THE HEART

Aorta

Pulmonary artery

FROM THE AORTA TO THE ARTIFICIAL HEART

Coronary artery

Inferior vena cava

Descending aorta

Sick Heart

In order for the heart transplant to take place, the heart must be stopped. This is achieved by reducing the body temperature of the patient. This has the benefit of also preserving the circulation of blood throughout the brain.

Donated heart

The donated heart must be the adequate size, taking into account the beneficiary's needs. In general, when a donor has an average weight and height, his or her heart most probably will work well on the majority of heart-transplant beneficiaries.

Heart Transplant

Heart transplant is, in general, the preferred treatment for heart failure when it is deemed that the possibility of survival and the quality of life cannot improve with any other traditional therapeutic alternative. The problem lies in establishing when other medical options should be discarded on the basis of this criterion. According to the American Heart Association, the clearest indications that such a transplant must be carried out are: cardiogenic shock, severe symptoms of ischemia that limit daily activity, and ventricular arrhythmias.

1 THE INCISION
Once the patient is under the effects of the anesthesia, the surgeon carries out an incision in the middle of the patient's chest and proceeds to open up the sternum. He then opens the pericardium until the sick heart is left in plain view.

2 PUMP
Once the pulmonary and cardiac functions of the patient have been substituted by an external artificial pump, called a heart-lung machine, the aorta is clamped. This is the doctor's cue for the heart exchange to happen.

LEFT VENTRICLE

RIGHT VENTRICLE

EXIT
The graft is considered to be successful when the new heart contracts forcefully and evenly.

3 EXTRACTION AND INSERTION OF DONOR HEART
The surgeon then removes the sick heart, separating it from the aorta and the pulmonary arteries. He then inserts the donated heart in its place. He sutures the left atrium in first, then sutures the septum, continuing all the way to the rim of the right atrium wall.

4 RESTORATION OF BLOOD FLOW
The pulmonary artery and the aorta are sutured to the donor heart. The aorta must be unclamped at this time. The surgeon checks for possible bleeding, and if the thermal and hemodynamic condition of the patient so permit, he proceeds to disconnect the patient from the artificial heart-lung machine.

5 INTENSIVE CARE
With the help of drainage tubes, the surgeon proceeds to close the breast incision. Finally, the patient, under constant surveillance, is transported to the intensive care unit. Once the postoperative period is over, the patient is released and begins a supervised ambulatory program in which he or she resumes physical movement such as walking.

iver Transplant

People who suffer advanced, irreversible, life-threatening hepatic conditions now have the ssibility of attempting a liver transplant. The most ical liver transplant cases are those of people who fer chronic hepatitis or primary biliary cirrhosis, an oimmune disease. Patients must not be infected in way and cannot be suffering from any cardiac or monary disease at the time.

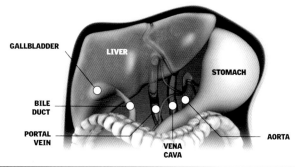

GALLBLADDER

LIVER

STOMACH

BILE DUCT

PORTAL VEIN

VENA CAVA

AORTA

1 DONATED LIVER
The organ, along with all its blood vessels and its bile duct, is removed immediately after the death of the donor.

2 THE NEW LIVER
is fused with the vena cava and the rest of the blood vessels. The opposite ends of the bile duct are sutured. A probe is inserted inside the reconstructed bile duct to drain the blood and the bile.

Artificial Organs

The search for alternative solutions to save human lives has reached its maximum development thus far with the construction of artificial organs. The AbioCor artificial heart is currently being improved, and it is expected that by 2008 it will have a useful life of five years. Similarly bionics has made it possible for blind persons to perceive images through impulses transmitted to the brain by video footage from a camera that acts as a retina. ●

The Development of Bionics

Advancements in bionics have begun to fulfill the wish that has been searched for in recent years: artificial organs literally identical to the natural ones—that is, organs that will not come with a limited useful life like other electronic devices. The world has already witnessed 16 successful bionic eye implants, and bionic arms are currently under development. Jesse Sullivan, the first bionic man, is able to control his artificial arms with his brain: the nerves of the lost arms were embedded in his chest, and when the patient thinks about closing his fist, a portion of the muscles in his chest contract, and the electrodes that detect the muscle activity "tell" the bionic arm to close the fist.

A BIONIC EYE
A microchip is placed at the back of the human eye. It is connected to a miniature video camera, which captures images that the chip later processes. The information is then sent as impulses to the brain, which interprets them.

ARMS
Today surgeries for prosthetics are common. The possibility of implanting joints that could be controlled by the brain was achieved with the case of Jesse Sullivan in 2001.

ARTIFICIAL KIDNEY
Research to improve dialysis is still active. The patient is connected to a machine that removes impurities and toxic elements from the blood in the event of renal failure.

Machines of Life

There are currently machines that can replace damaged bodily functions. Scientific developments and advances in bionics have created devices that can functionally replace organs with great effectiveness. The successful development of these machines has allowed organ activity to be restored in patients who would otherwise have lost it forever. The clear disadvantage of these devices, however, is that the patient must be permanently attached to the machine in order to avoid any risk. To overcome this limitation, organ transplants are being sought more and more frequently. The latest medical advancements led to the creation of artificial organs, such as the artificial lung and heart, which can perform essential functions of a patient's body without requiring him/her to be connected to a bulky machine.

ARTIFICIAL LUNG
It consists of an intravenous device that permits breathing. It is inserted in a vein in the leg and is later positioned inside the vena cava, the largest vein for blood return to the heart. Fibrous membranes introduce oxygen into the body and remove carbon dioxide from it. Although not intended for prolonged use, it helps provide information that can guide future studies.

Heart 2006
The AbioCor heart was designed especially to support a patient's circulatory system and to prolong the lives of people who would otherwise die from cardiovascular failure. The heart, developed by Abiomed, is completely implantable in the body.

Artificial Heart

AbioCor was a milestone in the development of the artificial heart. Unlike its predecessor, the Jarvik-7, AbioCor is the first mechanical heart that can be totally self-contained in the patient's body. It functions almost exactly the same as a natural heart. It has two ventricles and two valves that regulate blood circulation. The AbioCor heart is powered without the need for cables or tubes that pass through the patient's body.

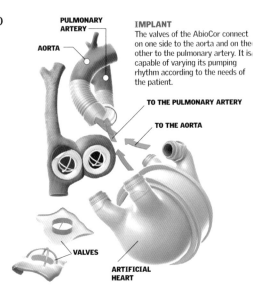

PULMONARY ARTERY

AORTA

IMPLANT
The valves of the AbioCor connect on one side to the aorta and on the other to the pulmonary artery. It is capable of varying its pumping rhythm according to the needs of the patient.

TO THE PULMONARY ARTERY

TO THE AORTA

VALVES

ARTIFICIAL HEART

HISTORY OF THE ARTIFICAL HEART

1 JARVIK-7
Robert Jarvik designed the first artificial heart, which was placed inside a patient in 1982. The Jarvik-7 functioned with an external air compressor, which provided power.

JARVIK-7

2 ABIOCOR
Unlike its predecessor, the AbioCor does not require an external power source. It was the first artificial heart to be fully implanted into a patient. It is still being developed, and scientists are attempting to extend its useful life to five years. It has already been authorized for use in the United States.

PUMPING SYSTEM

The heart developed by Abiomed is based on a hydraulic pump located at the center. Powered by a battery, the artificial heart reproduces the natural heart's performance almost identically. The deoxygenated blood goes to the lungs, and the oxygenated blood goes to the body.

AORTA

ONE-WAY VALVES

FLEXIBLE MEMBRANES

1 TO THE LUNGS
The blood lacking in oxygen flows to the lungs. It is pushed by a hydraulic pump and two membranes.

2 TO THE BODY
The oxygen-rich blood flows to the body. A cardiac rhythm is established to pump the blood according to the needs of the patient.

Abiocor Heart

is made up of two ventricles with valves. Each ventricle pushes 2 gallons (8 l) of blood a minute and emits 100,000 beats in a day. The right ventricle pushes the blood toward the lungs, and the left one pushes it toward the rest of the vital organs and the body. The operation of the mechanical heart replicates that of a natural heart. It is made of titanium and plastic.

5

WITHOUT INCISIONS
The transcutaneous energy transfer (TET) system allows the battery to transfer energy to an internal battery through the skin. This way, potential infections caused by maintaining an opening in the abdomen are avoided.

2

INTERNAL BATTERY
recharges directly from the external battery. It allows the patient a certain degree of autonomy, since it can run for an hour and a half without needing to connect to the external battery at the waist.

3

4

CONTROL SYSTEM
regulates the rhythm with which the artificial heart pumps the blood. Depending on the needs of the patient, it can be increased or decreased. The internal control system is an electronic device capable of detecting any type of anomaly and making it known so that the patient can act on it.

EXTERNAL BATTERIES
prevent the use of tubes, and the patient does not have to be immobilized. This source of power eliminates the need to connect to external machines to recharge the batteries. The device is worn at the waist and is portable.

1

Nanomedicine

The prefix "nano" indicates the scale on which the latest scientific developments are taking place: one billionth of a meter. From nanotechnology, advances have appeared in what is called nanomedicine. The main objective of this variant of nanotechnology is to obtain cures for diseases from inside the body and at a cellular or molecular level. Devices smaller than the diameter of a human hair have even been developed. ●

Nano-scaffolds for Regenerating Organs

The latest developments regarding the possibility of creating organs starting from a patient's own cells have demonstrated that by 2014 it may be possible to obtain a natural kidney simply through cellular regeneration rather than through a transplant. Beginning with biodegradable nanomolds, different organs could be created. The latest developments were able to produce a regenerated bladder in 1999. After being created, it was implanted successfully in seven patients. The procedure was done by doctor Anthony Atala of Wake Forest University. A section of a kidney that secretes a substance similar to urine has already been produced. Millions of nephrons still need to be regenerated, however, to achieve a fully functional kidney.

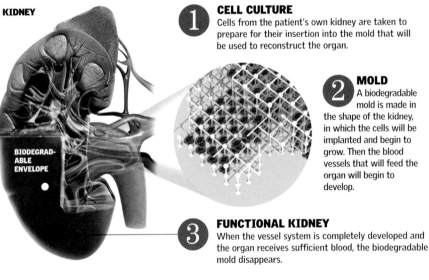

KIDNEY

BIODEGRADABLE ENVELOPE

1 CELL CULTURE
Cells from the patient's own kidney are taken to prepare for their insertion into the mold that will be used to reconstruct the organ.

2 MOLD
A biodegradable mold is made in the shape of the kidney, in which the cells will be implanted and begin to grow. Then the blood vessels that will feed the organ will begin to develop.

3 FUNCTIONAL KIDNEY
When the vessel system is completely developed and the organ receives sufficient blood, the biodegradable mold disappears.

Reconnecting Neurons

A group of scientists have developed a technique that allows nerve cells to regenerate. Chains of amino acids one thousandth the size of a red blood cell are used. Injected into the brain, these nanoparticles form a network over which the axons can stretch out and the connections may be able to be restored.

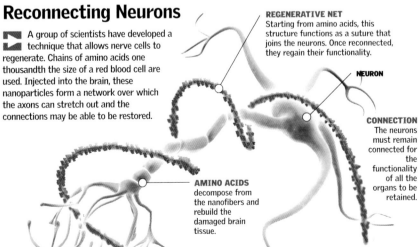

REGENERATIVE NET
Starting from amino acids, this structure functions as a suture that joins the neurons. Once reconnected, they regain their functionality.

NEURON

CONNECTION
The neurons must remain connected for the functionality of all the organs to be retained.

AMINO ACIDS
decompose from the nanofibers and rebuild the damaged brain tissue.

Nanotechnology

By working at the scale of a nanometer (10^{-9} meters), nanotechnology can currently be used in numerous areas of electronics, optics, and biomedicine. This state-of-the-art development builds devices so small that they can only be measured on the molecular scale. Today the most important and safest advances are the nanodevices used to detect cancer in its early stages. The nanoparticles can be between 100 and 10,000 times smaller than a human cell. Their size is similar to that of the larger biological molecules, such as enzymes. Nanoparticles smaller than 50 nanometers can easily enter any cell, while those smaller than 20 nanometers can move outside the blood vessels and circulate throughout the body.

MICROSCOPIC MOTOR
1 Smaller in diameter than a hair and 100 times thinner than a sheet of paper, micromotors are the basis for tiny machines that could travel through the body and destroy tumors or bacteria in their paths.

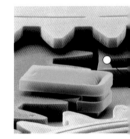

NANOTUBES
2 Nanotubes are structures whose diameter is on the order of a nanometer and whose length reaches up to a millimeter. They are the most resistant fibers known, between 10 and 100 times stronger than steel.

CARBON NANOTUBE

ELEMENTAL FORM
Like graphite and diamond, nanotubes are basic form of carbon. They are used in heavy industry

NANOTECHNOLOGIC MOLECULE
3 Each sphere of the molecule represents an atom: carbon in yellow, hydrogen in green, and sulfur in orange. It is based on fullerenes.

CARBON **SULFUR** **HYDROGEN**

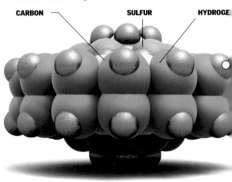

METER DECIMETER CENTIMETER MILLIMETER MICROMETER **NANOMETER** ANGSTROM PICOMETER FEMTOMETER ATTOMETER ZEPTOMETER YOCTOMETER

30,000 nanometers

Scales

Nanotechnologies can reach unimaginably small dimensions. The developments achieved to this day have been at the level of a micrometer, which corresponds to a fraction of a cell, and of a nanometer, which corresponds to a particle (about the size of five molecules of water) scale.

MILLIMETER
Equivalent to a thousandth of a meter. Abbreviated mm.

10^{-3}m

MICROMETER
Equivalent to a millionth of a meter. Abbreviated μm.

10^{-6}m

NANOMETER
Equivalent to a billionth of a meter. Abbreviated nm.

10^{-9}m

ANGSTROM
Equivalent to one ten billionth of a meter. Abbreviated Å.

10^{-10}m

A RELATIONSHIP OF SCALES
The relation between the diameter of a stem cell and that of a nanoparticle is similar in proportion between the relation between the diameter of a tennis ball and that of a small asteroid.

SIZE OF A CELL

20,000 Nanometers

EMBRYONIC STEM CELL

Nanoparticles

The use of nanoparticles to combat diseases such as cancer has been carried out successfully in rats by scientists Robert Langer and Omid Farokhzad. The nanoparticles are one thousandth the size of the period at the end of this sentence. They are made up of carbon polymers that directly attack the cancer cells and destroy them without harming surrounding healthy cells. They act like guided missiles. This approach would make it possible to surpass the complications of chemotherapy. It is estimated that its full development will be complete in 2014.

NANOPARTICLE

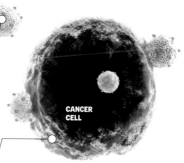

CANCER CELL

1 NANOSHIELDS
The small carbon "bombs" detect the cancer cells and go directly toward them. They adhere to the tumor and prepare for their second phase: unloading.

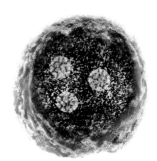

2 UNLOADING
Once the nanoparticles have entered the tumor, they release their carbon load, which contains instructions to destroy the cell.

DYING CELL

3 EXPLOSION
The attacked tumor cells are destroyed, and they die. Unlike chemotherapy, the surrounding healthy cells are not harmed.

NANOPARTICLES AND CELLS
To understand the scale at which nanoscopy works, we can compare the particles involved: a nanoparticle is to a cell what a grain of sand is to a football stadium.

A GRAIN OF SAND **IN A FOOTBALL STADIUM**

Nanoscopic Beams

Small microscopic and flexible beams that are built with semiconductors using lithographic techniques. These beams are covered with molecules capable of adhering to specific DNA. If a cancer cell secretes its molecular products, the antibodies placed on the flexible beams will bind to the secreted proteins. This generates a change in the physical properties of these beams, and researchers can read and interpret this information in real time.

CANCER CELL

1 ATTACK
The cancer cell secretes proteins to infect the organism.

PROTEINS

ANTIBODIES

CANCER CELLS

2 DEFENSE
The antibodies attract the proteins. The nanobeam varies and provides information about the presence of cancer.

NANOBEAMS

En Route to Eternity

The dream of an eternal body seems to dominate scientific study today. The possibility of building a nerve system from a network of cables, proposed through developments in neuroscience, and the building of metallic muscle systems are two examples of steps that are being taken in that direction. According to some specialists, the future promises the creation of a bionic body, without ties to flesh. In this scenario, every health problem could be solved though metallic implants. There is even a study that explores the possibility of repairing DNA after cell death to assure the eternal youth of cells. ●

DNA Repair

Biologist Miroslav Radman discovered that the bacteria *Deinococcus radiodurans* can be revived after being clinically dead, through the repair of its DNA. If DNA could be copied rapidly and the genome of dead human cells could be reconstructed, then the death of cells could be reversed, and all their organic functions could be restored: protein synthesis, lipids, and membranes.

Self-Healing Cells

The dream of having a body in which there is no degeneration of nerve cells is on its way to becoming a reality: neuroscientist John Donoghue of Brown University is trying to re-create the nervous system through optical fibers. These fibers would be used to transmit brain impulses. In the future, the body would be a perfect network of fibers that would be degeneration-proof. Any problem linked to the nerve system could be eliminated because the cables would substitute for the nerves.

Artificial Organs

Today efforts continue to design artificial organs that could replace organs that have been damaged or affected by severe diseases. By 2008, the Abiomed company plans to have the AbioCor heart developed to perfection. Although initial trials have been unsuccessful, Abiomed plans to design a heart that lasts for at least five years. Even so, it is very expensive: at least

ABIOCOR HEART

4,000
The number of stem-cell transplants worldwide

Organ Regeneration

Anthony Atala of Wake Forest University is the leading pioneer of organ-regeneration research. In 1999, he was able to re-create a bladder from cells extracted from other tissue. Atala and his team estimate that by 2014 great advancements will have occurred in the regeneration of the most complex organ: the kidney. Once a kidney can be regenerated, transplants and artificial organ implants will become a thing of the past.

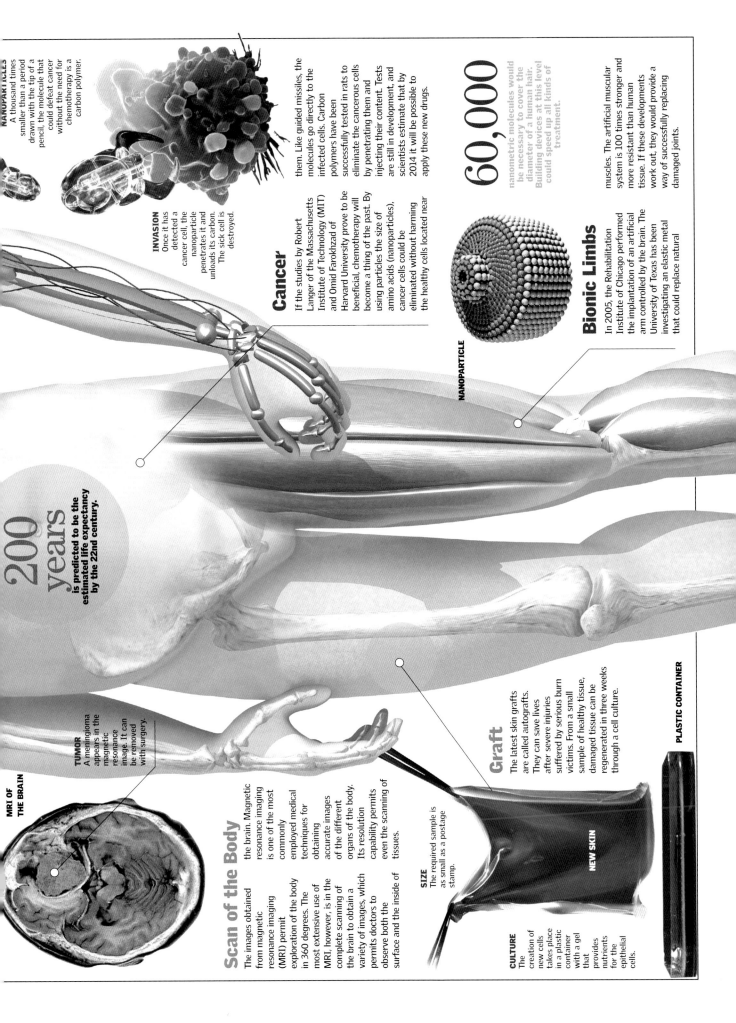

NANOPARTICLES

A thousand times smaller than a period drawn with the tip of a pencil, the molecule that could defeat cancer without the need for chemotherapy is a carbon polymer.

INVASION

Once it has detected a cancer cell, the nanoparticle penetrates it and unloads its content. The sick cell is destroyed.

Cancer

If the studies by Robert Langer of the Massachusetts Institute of Technology (MIT) and Omid Farokhzad of Harvard University prove to be beneficial, chemotherapy will become a thing of the past. By using particles the size of amino acids (nanoparticles), cancer cells could be eliminated without harming the healthy cells located near them. Like guided missiles, the molecules go directly to the infected cells. Carbon polymers have been successfully tested in rats to eliminate the cancerous cells by penetrating them and injecting their content. Tests are still in development, and scientists estimate that by 2014 it will be possible to apply these new drugs.

60,000

nanometric molecules would be necessary to cover the diameter of a human hair. Building devices at this level could speed up all kinds of treatment.

NANOPARTICLE

Bionic Limbs

In 2005, the Rehabilitation Institute of Chicago performed the implantation of an artificial arm controlled by the brain. The University of Texas has been investigating an elastic metal that could replace natural muscles. The artificial muscular system is 100 times stronger and more resistant than human tissue. If these developments work out, they would provide a way of successfully replacing damaged joints.

200 years

is predicted to be the estimated life expectancy by the 22nd century.

TUMOR

A meningioma appears in the magnetic resonance image. It can be removed with surgery.

MRI OF THE BRAIN

Scan of the Body

The images obtained from magnetic resonance imaging (MRI) permit exploration of the body in 360 degrees. The most extensive use of MRI, however, is in the complete scanning of the brain to obtain a variety of images, which permits doctors to observe both the surface and the inside of the brain. Magnetic resonance imaging is one of the most commonly employed medical techniques for obtaining accurate images of the different organs of the body. Its resolution capability permits even the scanning of tissues.

SIZE

The required sample is as small as a postage stamp.

Graft

The latest skin grafts are called autografts. They can save lives after severe injuries suffered by serious burn victims. From a small sample of healthy tissue, damaged tissue can be regenerated in three weeks through a cell culture.

CULTURE

The creation of new cells takes place in a plastic container with a gel that provides nutrients for the epithelial cells.

NEW SKIN

PLASTIC CONTAINER

Glossary

Agonist

Chemical product that, in addition to combining with a receptor (such as an antagonist), stimulates it, producing an observable effect. The term is also applied to a muscle that carries out a specific movement.

Allele

Variation of a gene in the population that codifies a specific trait. A diploid cell contains an allele from each parent for each characteristic.

Allergen

Substance or material capable of provoking an allergic reaction.

Alzheimer's Disease

A specific type of breakdown of the nervous system that causes cognitive disorders. It is related to advanced age.

Angiogenesis

Growth (normal or abnormal, depending on the circumstances) of new blood vessels in an organ or tissue.

Antagonist

Substance that inhibits or interferes with the action of other substances (hormones or enzymes). The term is also applied to muscles that, in the same anatomical region, act in opposite directions.

Antibiotic

Medicine that kills certain microorganisms or that impedes their growth and spread. It is used to treat infections.

Antigen

Substance that, when introduced into an animal body, results in defense reactions, such as the formation of antibodies.

Aorta

The largest artery in the body, it starts in the left ventricle of the heart. It is called the thoracic aorta until it reaches the diaphragm, and below that it is called the abdominal aorta, where it later bifurcates into the iliac arteries.

Arterial Hypertension

Elevated blood pressure, above 140 millimeters of mercury (systolic) and above 90 mm (diastolic).

Artery

Each one of the blood vessels through which the blood travels from the heart to supply the whole body.

Arthritis

Inflammation of the joint that could be the result of several causes.

Atherosclerosis

The accumulation of lipids (especially cholesterol) in the internal walls of the arteries; one of the main causes of diseases of the circulatory system.

Autonomous Nervous System

Part of the nervous system that regulates involuntary processes (heart rhythm, pupil dilation, stomach contractions, etc.). It includes the sympathetic and parasympathetic systems.

Bacterium

Microscopic organism that divides in two to reproduce. There are bacteria that are innocuous, pathogenic, and even beneficial to the human body.

Blastocyst

Cell mass, resulting from the division of the morula, that gives rise to the embryo.

Calcification

Fixation of calcium, an essential trace element for the formation of bones.

Cancer

Disease caused by the appearance and uncontrolled growth of a mass of abnormal tissue (malignant tumor).

Cell Membrane

Flexible envelope of all living cells that contains the cytoplasm. The membrane regulates the exchange of water and gases with the exterior.

Central Nervous System

Structure made up of the brain and the spinal cord.

Cerebral Cortex

Made up of gray matter present on the surface of the brain. It is the largest part of the central nervous system. Many of the most advanced functions take place in this cortex.

Cholesterol

Unsaturated lipid found in the body's tissues and in blood plasma. It is also found in elevated concentrations in the liver, spinal cord, pancreas, and brain. Cholesterol is ingested through some foods and is synthesized by the liver, then passed to the blood as HDL cholesterol, considered protective, or as LDL cholesterol, which in excess leads to the development of atherosclerosis.

Chromosome

Structure that carries the genes. These exist in the nucleus of each eukaryotic cell.

Cilia

Small cellular appendages shaped like hairs and used for locomotion in a liquid medium.

Conception

The union of a sperm with an egg.

Cytoplasm

Compartment in eukaryotic cells surrounded by the cell membrane.

Dermatophytosis

Infection in the skin caused by some species of fungi.

Diabetes

Chronic disease characterized by elevated levels of blood glucose due to metabolic disorders.

DNA

Deoxyribonucleic acid. Organic molecule with the shape of a double helix that contains the coded genetic information of an individual.

Dominance

Functional attribute of the genes by which they manifest their effect, regardless of the effect of the allele that accompanies them.

Embryo

Product of fertilization of the egg by a sperm; it can develop into an adult organism.

Endoplasmic Reticulum

Organelle made up of a network of membranes that joins the nucleus of a cell to the Golgi complex. Protein synthesis takes place in it.

Enzyme

Protein that helps to regulate the chemical processes of a cell, usually triggering or accelerating a reaction.

Erythrocytes

Red blood cells; they carry oxygen.

Estrogens

Female hormones produced by the ovaries and by the adrenal glands. They stimulate the growth of cells in the endometrium, the ovaries, and the breasts.

Fetus

The human body in gestation, after the third month and until birth.

Flagellum

Filament-like structure that is found on some bacteria and is used for locomotion.

Follicle

Sac-shaped gland located in the skin or in the mucous membranes.

FSH

Follicle stimulating hormone. Female hormone involved in the ovulation process.

Fungus

Live unicellular or multicellular organism belonging to the Fungi kingdom.

Gene

Information unit of a chromosome; the sequence of nucleotides in a DNA molecule that carries out a specific function.

Genome

The entire complex of chromosomes and their genes; the totality of the genetic material in a cell or individual.

Genotype

Genetic constitution of a single cell or an organism with reference to a single characteristic or set of characteristics; the sum of all the genes present in an individual.

Graft

Implantation into an organism of a portion of live tissue that comes from another organism or another part of the same one. Also, the portion of tissue to be implanted.

Hemoglobin

Protein (globin) associated with a porphyrin that contains iron (heme group) and is found inside the red blood cells; it transports oxygen.

Hormone

Product of gland secretion, its function is to stimulate, inhibit, or regulate the action of other glands, systems, or organs of the body.

Immune System

Set of processes centered on the blood and the lymphatic system that is activated to defend the human body against diseases.

Insulin

Hormone secreted by the pancreas that is responsible for the metabolism of glucose in the body.

Ion

Atom of an element or a molecule that is electrically charged because it has gained or lost electrons from its normal configuration.

Joint

The area where a bone or a skeletal organ comes together with another.

Laser

From the acronym for Light Amplification by Stimulated Emission of Radiation, it is a luminous artificial emission of variable frequency. Its energy can be controlled because of the coherence of its beams.

Leukocyte

White blood cell. A component cell of the blood, its main function is to defend the body from infectious agents.

Lipids

Organic chemical compounds formed mostly by hydrogen and carbon. Cholesterol and edible oils are the best known.

Lymph

Liquid that moves through the lymphatic system.

Lymphatic System

Ensemble of lymphatic vessels and ganglia that is independent of blood flow. It acts as a regulator of osmotic equilibrium in the body and as an activator of the immune system.

Lymphocyte

Belongs to the group of white blood cells. It is present in the blood and in the lymphatic system.

Lymphoma

Neoplastic disease that originates in the lymphatic system.

Meiosis

Type of cell division in which two successive cell divisions of the nucleus of a diploid cell result in four haploid nuclei. As a result of this mechanism, gametes or spores are produced.

Metabolism

Set of chemical reactions that are constantly carried out by cells to synthesize complex substances from simpler ones or to degrade the former to obtain the latter, as in the digestive process, for example. The activity level of body functions at rest and while fasting is called basal metabolism.

Metastasis

Spreading of a cancerous tissue, making it capable of attacking organs other than the one from which it originated.

Mitochondria

Organelle that is bounded by a double membrane. Within the mitochondria, ATP is obtained from the decomposition of sugars and other substances—the final step in aerobic respiration.

Mitosis

Division of a cell in which two identical cells are formed from the parent cell.

Morula

Early stage in the development of a multicellular organism, made up of 16 to 64 cells. It gives rise to the blastocyst.

Mycosis

Infection caused by fungi.

Nanotechnology

Industrial technology that permits the fabrication of microscopic devices.

Neurotransmitter

Chemical substances responsible for the transmission of the nerve impulse through neuron synapses.

Nucleus

Part of the cell inside the cytoplasm. The nucleus contains almost all the DNA in a cell.

Osmosis

Diffusion of water through a semipermeable membrane.

Ovulation

Release of the mature egg from the ovary through the fallopian tube.

Oxyhemoglobin

Hemoglobin of arterial blood that is loaded with oxygen.

Oxytocin

Female hormone produced by the hypothalamus, it is transported to the hypophysis and is later released into the bloodstream. In women, it is responsible for, among other functions, the milk-ejection reflex and uterine contractions.

Parkinson's Disease

Neurological disorder caused by a deficit of the neurotransmitter called dopamine.

Pectoral Angina

Oppressive pain located in the retrosternal region, caused by an insufficient flow of oxygenated blood to the cardiac muscle.

Phenotype

Physical expression of a genotype.

Platelet

Cellular component of blood that takes part in the clotting process.

Progesterone

Female hormone involved in the menstrual cycle and gestation.

Protein

Substance that makes up parts of the cells. It is formed by one or more chains of amino acids and is fundamental to the constitution and functioning of the essentials of life, such as enzymes, hormones, and antibodies.

Protozoa

Microscopic, unicellular, heterotrophic organisms that live in an aqueous medium and that reproduce through bipartition.

Reflex

Automatic and involuntary reaction of the nervous system that is produced in response to a stimulus.

Ribosome

An organelle located in the cytoplasm, it directs the formation of proteins based on the information given by the nucleic acids.

RNA

Ribonucleic acid, similar to DNA but used to transport a copy of the DNA to the ribosome, where proteins are manufactured.

Saturated Fats

Fats of animal origin that are involved in nutrition.

Schwann Cells

Cells that produce myelin, a fatty insulating substance; it covers the nerve fibers that keeps the electrical signals from losing speed as they get farther away from the body of the neuron.

Semen

Combination of sperm and liquid substances produced in the male genital system.

Somatotropin

Human growth hormone, secreted by the pituitary gland (hypophysis).

Spirillum

Flagellated bacterium with a helical or spiral form.

Spore

Reproductive cell of a fungus.

Sugar

Generic name of the organic chemical compounds known as carbohydrates.

Synthesis

Chemical process in which two or more molecules join to produce a larger one.

Systemic

Describes a disorder that affects several organs or the body as a whole.

Testosterone

Androgenic hormone related to the primary as well as secondary male sexual traits. It is produced by the testicles and to a lesser extent by the adrenal glands and ovaries in women.

Thrombus

Solid mass of blood formed inside a vein or artery. If it travels through the circulatory system, it is called an embolus, which can cause an obstruction.

Tissue

Group of identical cells that carry out a common function.

Transcription

Copying of the genetic code of the DNA into another molecule, such as RNA.

Transplant

Insertion of live tissue into a living organism from another organism (living or not).

Tumor

Any alteration of the tissues that produces an increase in volume.

Vagus Nerve

Also called the pneumogastric nerve, it is the 10th of the 12 cranial pairs. It originates in the brainstem and innervates the pharynx, esophagus, larynx, trachea, bronchia, heart, stomach, and liver.

Vein

Each one of the blood vessels that take deoxygenated blood to the heart.

Vibrio

Genus of elongated bacteria in the shape of a comma with a single cilium, such as the one that produces cholera.

Virus

Organism at the boundary between living and inert. It can be potentially pathogenic, and it can consist of a protein capsule (capsid) that surrounds the genetic material (DNA or RNA).

Vitamin

One of the organic substances that ensures the equilibrium of vital functions and constitution of the tissues. They are designated with the letters of the alphabet.

Zona Pellucida

Envelope that protects the egg; the sperm must negotiate it during fertilization.

Zygote

The diploid cell formed by the union of the sperm and the egg after fertilization; also called the ovum.

Index

uterine cervix, 51
candidiasis, 53
CD4-positive T lymphocyte, 76
cell division, mitosis, 11
cellular regeneration, 88
central nervous system
    Parkinson's disease, 63
    seven month embryo, 35
    sleeping sickness, 55
cephalic presentation, 36
cervix (uterine)
    cancer, 51
    childbirth, 41
cesarean section, 36
chest pain: *See* pectoral angina
chicken pox, 51
childbirth
    fetal presentation, 36, 37
    labor, 40-41
    pain management, 41
chorion, 14
chromosome
    amniocentesis, 28
    bacterial, 48, 49
    sex differentiation, 27, 45
chronic bronchitis, 68
circulatory disease, 66-67
circulatory system
    disease, 66-67
    four month embryo, 29
    newborn, 42
    umbilical cord, 33
cirrhosis, 70
clitoris, 26
coccus bacteria, 48
cochlea (ear), 32
cold weather allergy, 75
colitis, 73
colon
    cancer, 73
    diseases, 72, 73
    X-ray, 80
common cold virus, 51
computerized tomography (CT), 81
conidia: *See* sporangia

connective tissue, embryonic formation, 18
contact lens, 83
contraction: *See* childbirth
coronavirus, 51
Crohn's disease, 73
cryptococcosis, 53
cytosine, 44

D

defense system, 31
    See also immune system
degenerative disease
    bones, 64-65
    Parkinson's disease, 63
dendrite, 25
dengue, 51
dermatophytosis, 53
diabetes, gestational, 35
diagnosis, medical, 80-81
    See also specific terms, for example X-ray
digestive system
    AIDS effects, 76
    diseases, 70-73
dilation, childbirth, 40
Dinoire, Isabelle, 84
disease: *See organ systems and types of disease by name*
diverticulitis, 73
DNA
    bacterial, 48, 49
    bacteriophage, 50, 51
    fertilization, 11
    repair, 90
    structure, 44-45
    See also RNA
Donoghue, John, 91
dopamine, Parkinson's disease, 63
double helix: *See* DNA
drug: *See* medicine
dust mite, 75

dysplasia, 60

E

ear
    balance, 32
    eight month fetus, 37
    embryonic formation, 19, 20, 21
    fetal sound perception, 31
    four month fetus, 29
    structure, 32
economic development, allergy incidence, 74, 75
ectoderm, 13
egg, fertilization, 10-11
ejaculation (sperm), 8
elderly, the
    Alzheimer's disease, 62-63
    osteoarthritis, 64, 65
    osteoporosis, 65
    Parkinson's disease, 63
embryo
    formation, 13, 14-15, 16
    vertebrate similarities, 45
    See also specific organs, for example arm
encapsulated camera, 80
encephalitis, 51
endoderm, 13
endometrium, 13
endoparasite, 54-55
enzyme, AIDS progression, 76
epidural anesthesia, 41
Escherichia coli, 72
esophagus, embryonic formation, 16
eye
    artificial implant, 86
    early embryonic formation, 17, 19, 21
    eight month fetus, 37
    eyelid formation, 18, 19
    laser surgery, 82-83
    pupil, 82
    seven month fetus, 35

hypophysis: *See* **pituitary gland**

I-K

identical twin, 44
immune system
  allergies: *See* **allergy**
  antibiotic action: *See* **antibiotic**
  fetal development, 31
  red and white blood cells, 56
  rheumatoid arthritis, 65
  See also **AIDS; autoimmune system; white blood cell**
impulse transmission, 24, 25
industrialization, allergy incidence, 74, 75
infarction: *See* **heart attack**
inheritance, genetic, 44-45
integrase, 76
intestine
  infection, 72
  inflammation, 73
isograft, 84
Jarvik, Robert, 86
Jarvik-7 (artificial heart), 86
joint, degeneration, 64, 65
Kaposi's sarcoma, 76
kidney
  artificial organ, 86
  cellular regeneration, 88
  embryonic formation, 16

L

labor, childbirth, 40-41
lactation: *See* **milk production**
Lactobacillus acidophilus, 48
Langer, Robert, 89, 91
language disorder, 62
languo (fetal hair), 30

  disappearance, 36
laser surgery, 82-83
LASIK surgery, 83
leg
  embryonic bud formation, 18, 21
  four month fetus, 28
Legionella pneumophila, 68
leukemia, 51
life support system, 86
light, fetal reaction, 35, 37
liver
  artificial organ, 86
  cirrhosis, 70
  embryonic formation, 16
  function, 70, 71
  transplant, 85
lochia, postpartum processes, 43
lung
  AIDS effects, 76
  artificial organ, 86
  cancer, 61, 69
  embryonic formation, 16
  infections, 68-69
  newborn, 42
  structure, 69
  surfactant, 36
lymphocyte, 56
  CD4-positive T lymphocytes, 76
lyzosome, 51

M

magnetic resonance imaging (MRI), 80, 81
  brain scan, 91
  prenatal tests, 31
  See also **3D magnetic resonance imaging**
male reproductive system, 8
  karyotype, 45
  testicle, 28
  third month fetus, 26
  Y chromosome speed, 27
mammary gland, 38

  See also **milk production**
mammogram, 60
mast cell, 74
meconium, 36
medical informatics, 5
medical technology: *See specific terms, for example* **ultrasound**
medicine, 78-91
  bacterial infection: *See* **antibiotic**
  fetal monitoring, 28, 31
  fungal infection, 53
  HIV treatment, 77
memory loss, 62
men
  cancers, 61
  Parkinson's disease, 63
  prostate cancer, 61
  sex differentiation, 26, 45
  See also **male reproductive system**
meningitis, 53
menopause, 8
menstrual cycle, 9, 39
mesoderm, 13
metastasis, 60, 61
metric measurement, 89
micromotor, 88
microtubule, 62
milk production, 38
  hormones, 43
mitosis, 11
monocyte, 56
morphogen, 14
morphogenesis, 14
morula, 12
multiple sclerosis, 63
Mycobacterium tuberculosis, 46-47
myelin envelope, 24, 25
  multiple sclerosis, 63
myopia, laser surgery, 83